THE WORLD HATE CRISIS:

THROUGH THE EYES
OF A DREAM PSYCHIC

Ann Marie Ruby

DEDICATION

THE WORLD LEADERS OF ALL

Sacred be the sacrifices

Of the sacred souls.

From dawn through dusk,

Throughout the storms,

And through

The unknown and unseen paths,

You be the guide

For you but lead,

As we but follow.

Never do you fall.

For your love for all,

We the citizens say in union,

You but create a blessed

Sacred haven we call

Our home, our land, our country,

Our one Earth.

For you are known to one,

And to all,

As you have the sacred blessed souls,

Who but eradicate

The World Hate Crisis.

You are but blessed to be,

THE WORLD LEADERS OF ALL.

TABLE OF CONTENTS

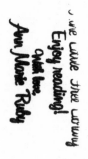

MESSAGE FROM THE AUTHOR

"Sacred messages spread throughout time become history through the pen and the paper."

-Ann Marie Ruby

Land after land was going through depression. Houses were being foreclosed. I walked with The Holy Spirit and cried for all the unknown faces of depression. Something had converted a small crisis into a catastrophic world crisis. I asked my Lord, "What is going on?" I knew all around, people were talking about the hate crisis.

In my dream, was the frightening vision of what this world would but face. I knew the future looked bleak as the rich just got richer and all others of the land suffered. I knew I must do something.

I saw world leaders had gathered for an Emergency Alert situation. There were sirens going off throughout the lands and something was not right. I saw a huge red warning signal. People were scattered all around.

Overnight, something had converted this one world, our home, into a place everyone wanted to escape from. Where do we go and hide if our world, our Heaven, but becomes our Hell? I heard the world leaders talk about how all of this had begun with the instigators of the hate crisis.

Hitler, with his powerful energy of hatred, was successful in taking so many lives. What would a similar group of people be capable of, especially if they have within their hands, the weapons of mass destruction? Again, I knew I must do something.

I saw fire fall from the skies down onto Earth as a curse had befallen upon the humans. I was praying and I asked my Lord, "But why?" This fire shall burn down all the humans without them even realizing. Why were the humans being cursed? I knew land after land had converted into ashes and all the people were fighting amongst each other, arguing over who was right and who was wrong.

I asked all of the people, "Have any one of you died and come back? Do you know the beyond? Then, why is your voice so loud? Why are you putting down your neighbors for being different?" I asked all to find peace within themselves and let peace spread, not the hate crisis.

I had awakened with this nightmare of the hate crisis. I knew the seers of the past had seen this prophecy. They had seen buildings were being crushed or burned down. They did not realize the truth. Yes, the buildings and houses were being burned down through the hate crisis. The fire burning within the human souls is but what shall burn down the human race. We must act now and extinguish this fire.

Through my eyes, come and walk with me as we see *The World Hate Crisis*. This book is my warning for all of the present and the future as we have not paid heed to the past seers. This book is a guide as to what we need to do to avoid this catastrophic situation.

As a dream psychic, I believe in prophecies, but I also believe in dreams. The difference between myself and others is that I believe in walking with the truth, within the paths of the philosophers, the religious scholars, and the scientific scholars in union.

Dreams are given for guidance, not as a threat, but as a blessing. Dreams guide us as to what to avoid, where not to go, and how to deal with a situation. A doctor would say preventive measures are taken to avoid a situation. As a diabetic, I have to control my food intake and must take my daily medication. I had no clue I was diabetic even though I had been to the doctor.

I had a dream in which I was very sick and was asked to go into the emergency room right away. The next morning, I visited the emergency room and now I am on medication for diabetes. My dream had guided me to this situation. I had to go and hold the helping hands of the scientific scholars as I am not a magical healer, but a practical person.

I must walk the walk to find my destination. For now, I want all the world leaders to unite and find a way out of this situation the world shall find herself within. It is not long before this storm but becomes a world crisis. Hate crimes are not new. All of the world citizens know it is we the humans who are in the process of becoming extinct if we do not pay heed to this situation.

You the citizen change yourself, do your share in eradicating *The World Hate Crisis*, and unite with me. I believe this is a crisis we the united citizens should not ignore at this stage of human existence. History testifies we have had political and social instigators of hate crimes for which World War II had intensified. These hate crimes increased the number of lives that were taken away from us far before their time.

The Second World War, and all the reported and unreported crimes of the present time tell us a story. We might just be heading toward the Third World War if we do not stop the increasing number of hate crimes. The instigators only see their perspective, not the perspectives of those who are different from them. The warnings of the past seers have warned us of these upcoming catastrophic changes yet to come within the lives of the present and future generations. For this reason, I have taken pen to paper, the only tool I the unknown person but have to do something for you and all the future generations yet to come. Let us in union eradicate this crisis before this crisis but eradicates us the humans.

As I stood in Het Plein, the town square, in The Hague, the Netherlands, watching the statue of William the Silent, I felt I had a connection with him. When I visited his home in Delft, the Netherlands, it is then I realized this was the person I had seen in my dreams. I never realized the connection between the orange tree and William the Silent, both from my dreams, until I walked into his home.

My dreams of William the Silent had come to life in front of me. I was walking within the home of a person I walked with so many times within my dreams. Yet, here I am in the present days, and I know William the Silent was before my time. Miracles are just that, pure miracles. His life story teaches us he had the wisdom and courage to stand up for different faiths and freedom of religion. At a time when people were scared to voice their difference of opinions, he had spoken out for all. The citizens of the Netherlands would be proud and blessed to call him their father.

I only wish he was my father too. I know I will honor him and his blessed footsteps. I know the connection is there as I too want this world to be one home for all of her citizens with different views, who are of different race, color, and religion. Standing on the land where William the Silent still rests, I promised I too will follow his dream, and my blessed dreams.

The weather forecast as I had traveled to the Netherlands was to be rainy every single day. Should I have canceled my trip or just continue as I had planned? I chose to continue with caution. I bought an umbrella and rain gear, but I continued my trip. A seer guides. You should never stop your life, your way, or your journey, but it is always better to walk with caution. You never know the path you are traveling upon may have bumps and obstacles that just appear or were but predicted to appear.

As a dream psychic, I rely on my memories of the dreams of the past. As I awaken to dawn, I only have the reminiscence of the previous night's dreams. How do I interconnect the dreams to the everlasting truths of the daylight hours? Within the daylight hours, all seem clear as evidence is but found throughout time.

All but become clear within time as there is always a hidden message within each dream. We receive messages through dreams or through the voices of historical figures as their words become history. It is then, these words become our saving grace for they are the first sign of dawn through the dark night skies.

Today, I walk within the same path of humanity that was left behind for us through the historical figures of the past. I have wondered why The Holy Spirit would over and over again, show me dreams of the world, the crises she but suffers, and the suffering of humans. Within my dreams, I have seen various world leaders trying to resolve the crises our one world but faces. How do I ignore the suffering and pain of the beloved creation of The Creator? How do I but remain silent?

I believe in the famous words that have been attributed to Gautama Buddha, "Three things cannot be long hidden: the sun, the moon, and the truth." The truth is that the suffering of the victims of hate crimes can only be eradicated when we all but unite. Personally, I believe within the humans, we have angels in disguise. I have met one individual who is known to all of you as a world leader, yet to this soul, he is my hope that within all world leaders, there is but hidden a human with humanity.

There is a leader from a different land and different culture, whose personal, political, or social life I have no clue about, yet through the miracles of life, this person was introduced to me.

Do you believe in miracles?
Do you have faith in God?
Do you believe in dreams?

My answer to all of the above is, "Yes, I do." From beyond the human comprehension or understanding, there is a door to the miracles of the beyond. Through this door of miracles, I let my personal dreams guide me to this individual. Through my own research, always being guided by my personal dreams, I have found the courage to write about a human who was introduced to me through my sacred dreams. I write about this person from my very personal perspective, as I was guided by only my dreams, not by his words or his way of life.

I have not actually interviewed him, nor do I know his perspectives, be it personal, political, or social. Travel with me through these pages as I share only my personal view of a person who had my faith and respect grow within all world leaders. This person has given me hope to believe all the world leaders in union shall eradicate the biggest crisis that has but dawned upon us.

You all know him by his given name, Prime Minister of the Netherlands, Mark Rutte. As I have seen how modestly this one man but lives and walks amongst all the world leaders, I believe in all of them. From afar, all look like strangers; however, when you see them with an open mind, you see humans with humanity.

I ask you the individual to ask all the world leaders to unite and help eradicate this invisible, yet painful crisis that but brews amongst us. May we the individual citizens in union with each respective world leader be able to free this Earth from this world crisis that but brews forcefully. The citizen and the leader, let us walk hand in hand and protect all as we become the glowing hope within these dark times.

May my message reach all the unknown doors of the known sacred leaders of this world. Please stand in union, world citizens and leaders, as I give to you my book,

THE WORLD HATE CRISIS:
THROUGH THE EYES OF A DREAM PSYCHIC.

INTRODUCTION

"The first breath of dawn but introduces herself to all, as she steps into our lives with miracles and blessings."

-Ann Marie Ruby

Dawn brings hope to this world as darkness but evaporates like the early morning dew. Life is a blessing as we finally find ourselves within the first morning glory. I have planted morning glories throughout my garden as the symbol of an answered prayer of a sacred soul.

I love to take midnight strolls through my twenty-acre property within the foothills of Mount Rainier. As the natural pond reflects the glowing light from the moon above, I feel like I can jump into the pond and touch the moon through the glass mirrors of the water. She shines upon the dark world, glorifying her miracle as she reflects light to all that come upon her path.

As I watch the stars reflecting upon my pond, I know these are the angels who had walked on Earth as humans. Different in shade and size they all look, yet I know they were multinational and multicultural lives lost because they were but different from their attackers. They blink upon the night skies asking for justice. They watch as more and more lives fade away from the Earth to this catastrophic war, invisible to the eyes of the humans, yet visibly brewing within the inner souls of the perpetrators.

Today, within your blessed hands, light a candle to keep the memories glowing, for they are but our guiding stars guiding all humans through their lives lived. They but shed tears from the skies above for justice. All over this world, we have humans who also glow upon the dark nights like the stars above, burning for all whom but seek their blessings.

Throughout time, this world gives birth to these humans who walk within the same path you and I but walk upon, yet they become a lighthouse for all whom but need their guidance. History guides us to them through the wheels of time. After living a life to only keep the lanterns burning for all of the known and unknown travelers of life, they leave us only to become historical figures. I know history has good and bad tales through the lives lived of the human travelers, still walking upon the pages of history. Some of these historical figures have guided us and some have made history by misleading others.

I seek the good within all individual souls, for I believe humans are interconnected through humanity. I know each story recited by a witness is but the personal perspective of the perceived. Stories get lost through the time tunnels of life. As dawn approaches, I ask myself, why do I seek answers that are not within my reach? Why do I hear cries from voices that have not knocked upon my door?

I pray may I be blessed to wake up at dawn to find the sacred world leaders, united and walking to resolve all of my unanswered questions as they too feel for the humans of this world. I wondered about these questions for many years. I finally decided to write my book, my personal perspective, my personal journey through my dreams, and the life journey of the humans and the world leaders who but walk upon this Earth with honor, courage, and dignity. I call these people, humans with humanity.

I wanted a sign from the above to guide me within this sacred journey. This world is under attack from us the humans through our innermost feelings of division. I asked myself if the world leaders look upon this crisis and realize it is time they too get involved. It is not a health crisis. For the health crisis, we have medical teams and international organizations throughout this world putting in their efforts to eradicate all health issues. It is not the climate crisis. For the climate crisis, we have the scientists guiding us what to do and what to avoid. It is not the world food crisis. For the world food crisis, we have international organizations trying to battle this war.

We have landed upon a time when *The World Hate Crisis* is but knocking upon our doors. I know if this world is infested with a great disease known as *The World Hate Crisis*, then there are some world leaders who shall awaken to eradicate this obstacle. I know there are some leaders who can resolve this problem as their journey but testifies they can achieve this goal.

We need you, the world leader, and I, the individual, to unite and resolve this crisis. The humans are but lost within this storm. If we do not give a helping hand to each other, then for whom and what are we saving this one world? We cannot awaken the world leaders without all of our united voices. When we the individuals awaken and call upon the leaders in union, it is then we are but noticed. One voice gets lost in this brewing storm, but when we the individuals unite and are louder than the brewing storm, it is then we shall be victorious.

Alexander the Great famously said, "I am not afraid of an army of lions led by a sheep; I am afraid of an army of sheep led by a lion" ("Alexander the Great"). I call upon a human with humanity to awaken and lead for a cause you but believe in. Let all the world leaders follow your cause and let humanity be the final leader for the human race throughout eternity. World leaders are sacred souls, who are there only to guide us out from the catastrophic storms of life, and to be a candle of hope when all but get dark.

I admire what Nelson Mandela, a great world leader, had written, "A leader ... is like a shepherd. He stays behind the flock, letting the most nimble go out ahead, whereupon the others follow, not realizing that all along they are being directed from behind" (22). My inspiration comes through these sacred words from the past. World leaders throughout time have placed themselves on the world stage, for it is their chosen path. The question that arrives within my mind is but why?

It is then, you are but open to all the critics and their harsh criticism. The unjust voices echo all around you, yet only a few days ago, these were the voices of praise that had walked with you. I know you the great leaders known to all throughout time as sacred people but hold on to the hands of a supporter and an opponent.

Again I ask, but why? Why did the love and support disappear? Why is it when you do not know someone, you admire the footsteps of the person? Yet, why is it when the person is in front of you, you want someone different? Why is it your admired but becomes an admired no more? I ask you to admire the work, not the person. Admire what the person is capable of doing, not whether or not he or she is but your chosen one.

It is true perspectives change as the clouds clear and you see the dust lying around that was but invisible before. Upon close inspection, you realize the dust was always there, but it was you who chose not to see. Admire with or without the dust, for is there a human amongst the creation who has no dust upon him or herself? Historical and Biblical testimonies but testify the same.

I believe if a person gives up his or her personal freedom to serve his or her country, then this is a virtue we must respect, even given our personal differences. The path may be different, and the travelers are all different, but the journey through this life is the same. Throughout the journey of life, we find out the good and bad intentions of a person, as the person but becomes history. Life is a lesson learned, through the individual life lived.

Within this book, I talk about the lives that left too early before we the society were ready to bid our goodbyes. The truth is being buried within the Earth as are the victims. This Earth is my mother as all the humans are but my siblings, so I the sister must speak up for the victims of these catastrophic crimes. The hidden crimes of the perpetrators, which are unseen, unknown, and unheard to you the stranger, shall be known as daylight but approaches.

Throughout this book, I talk about my personal perspective. I feel we have landed upon a time period when hate crimes have increased because the instigators of these crimes are openly inviting people. The invitees never thought they would openly get involved in these crimes for their feelings were buried deep within.

As more and more instigators are openly attacking victims, however, the group of attackers is increasing in size. Religious and social differences are also providing bait to the instigators who are using these sensitive issues to divide all. Reported crimes and unreported crimes are also a factor within the statistics, as some are being reported yet a lot of crimes are still not reported.

Temptation is a known and forbidden sin. If everyone is engaging within this act, however, you feel like it must be okay because everyone is involved. A woman had argued with me on this topic. I had asked her, "Why would a person knowingly sin?" She tried to convince me by asking, "How many humans would your God place in Hell if all the people are sinning?" I knew there was no point in arguing with her. She thought her voice was right as she had a lot of followers who made fun of me. I walked out of this group knowing it was not the right group, but would you be able to walk out of a group you were born or forced into?

CHAPTER ONE

FOOTSTEPS

"The human race has one color, one kind, and is but one group, unless you are the ignorant eye, for then you can only see yourself within the mirror. I but see myself within the eyes of all humans. The reflections left behind shall be imprinted throughout time as all but reflect upon the path created by the beholders of the sacred footsteps."

-Ann Marie Ruby

Within the sand, we the humans see footprints left behind by the past travelers. Within my dreams, I but see the footsteps of the future travelers. Hold my hands and let us in union create a wishing well where we can catch the teardrops of all. Ignorance is a virtue until you are the one who but needs attention.

Build a wall to ignore the teardrops of your neighbors until the teardrops but flood your home. It is then, your same neighbor carries you to safety as he had built a canoe for these catastrophic days. Be the neighbor who gives for humanity, not the one who but builds a wall to only separate all humans from humanity. Today, I watch all the teardrops of the victims affected by hate crimes flood this world, the same Earth that but was formed from love and harmony.

My Earth is a peaceful and serene place where colorful rainbows appear and disappear to please the humans. The carpets created completely out of colorful flowers, blossom to remind us that differences are what make this Earth beautiful. Earth is where we the humans walk in union for climate control, for gun control, where vegetarians like myself walk for animal rights, and now I walk for human rights too. Hate crimes have spiked throughout this world, as the prejudicial acts of individuals have created division within our one Earth.

Individual inner hatred of a person or a group, toward another individual or group for being different, is but the personal aggression of the perpetrators. The only intention they have within their souls, is to inflict physical or emotional harm toward an innocent human, for being different. How low have we the humans sunk, that we force to be the superior group and decide the rest are inferior as we the perpetrators are the might? How much more do we the humans want our Mother Earth to suffer? The humans are mortal, yet their sins have become immortal through the actions of their own taking.

I had written a prayer in which I compared the human life to a day. We know dawn is the start and as nightfall approaches, all but shall end. Then I ask, why do you write history with your negative activities? The human race is in grave danger of extinguishing each other as we engage in the most catastrophic war of all time. I call this invisible war we are in the midst of, *The World Hate Crisis*.

I am a person with love and honor for all humans. I call this my humanity. I know I am not a leader or even known to anyone. For my inner love of the one human race,

I have become a humanitarian who shall walk with you, for you, as we in union find a solution to this crisis. For you the humans, I will now place my footsteps within the pages of history, as I begin my own war to eradicate *The World Hate Crisis.*

My thoughts drift to the world leaders and their footsteps, as I believe footsteps laid by a leader upon the nation are but imprinted within history throughout time. Who are the world leaders and what are their impacts upon the human race? Throughout time, there is always a person leading a group to safety or into a ditch.

Life is a journey where we the humans but follow the leaders. At all times, upon the shoulders of these people are the burdens of the truth and safety of all that but follow. We must remember we the citizens with the power vested within us, elect our leaders to lead us. We also have the power to reject the world leaders as the foremost concern was, is, and shall always be human rights.

Following a leader is but a blessing or a curse that only the mirrors of life shall answer when you end up at the winning stage, or the pitfall of life. It is but the inspired who are the winners or losers as the end result is of your chosen path. Throughout time, historical figures but lead a nation or take a nation astray, as they rise or fall through their chosen path. It is we the citizens who choose our leaders. We must look down history and face her when she spreads tears through the written pages of her life, lived by us the citizens.

Our one Earth is now facing the biggest crisis that history shall record as an apocalyptic catastrophe for we the humans have failed to wipe the tears of our fellow humans. Today, aside from climate change, the human behavioral changes are directly impacting the human race through human hate crimes. From the first sight of dawn, through the first sight of dusk, and all throughout the dark nights, I carry the candles of hope within my hands, always watching out for a lost and stranded soul.

Life is full of obstacles where natural and unnatural calamities follow us the humans and our habitat, the Earth. Today, I stand upon this Earth immersed within the thoughts about all of the humans living across this globe. Where are we going to land one hundred years from now? We the present will not be there, but our actions will remain as footprints throughout this world for all future inhabitants. Leaders are but there to guide our vehicles to safety, even throughout the storms of life. This world is experiencing a crisis where we the citizens united with the world leaders must do our share.

I had seen how society has divided us by race and ethnicity when I tried to buy a house in New Orleans, Louisiana. I drove into a neighborhood and saw an open house on a Sunday afternoon. I loved talking to some neighbors who had invited me inside for tea, as I had stopped and inquired about a house for sale. I absolutely loved the house and the neighborhood. I called my agent to inquire and get all the information on the house.

My agent, however, advised me not to buy the house as it was in a predominantly black neighborhood. Her advice was to buy a house in a different neighborhood, where there was less of a racial division. I could not believe her comments and how she had gone on and on about the division amongst different races and ethnicities. Her point of view as she explained to me was that the racial division was not her problem.

I found myself another agent the following day. I eventually bought another house as the house I had set my heart on had sold within hours. I did live in a multicultural New Orleans neighborhood and had never felt the racism or racial differences between neighbors. I had neighbors who brought baked dishes over to my house on weekends. I had always wondered were people pretending to be nice to each other? Or were people really growing to like each other? Interracial marriages were blooming in my neighborhood and had renewed my faith within the human race.

Why is society becoming more divided now rather than more diverse? Hate crimes have increased to such a level that within this technological world where we should be uniting, we are instead bullying and dividing even through cyberspace. I see the divisions have sparked another stage within our one world. Please do not be the person who but takes away a child from the hands of a mother. I hope and pray we can all walk above this period and unite for each other.

I know I have no clue what to do, or where to start, so I too can do my share of small things around the house, or within my neighborhood, or my city, then within my country. I know united we can solve this problem as when humans unite, we are but the biggest force in existence. I pray for the world leaders to unite and may they be victorious. Invisible it may seem to some eyes, but to the eyes of the future, this will be a blessing left behind. They too can enjoy the Earth like we are enjoying today.

I know we have a health crisis, climate crisis, and food crisis, which are all huge issues as are so many other crises, growing each and every day. The world leaders are trying to tackle these issues as they gather in union and collect you the individual's personal experiences. As all the crises but evolve all around us, I know there is a crisis brewing amongst us that also needs to be resolved.

This crisis, however, is but brewing within individuals as a wild storm, a nightmare catching on throughout this world. This is an invisible force, yet very contagious as she is but stronger than any war that we the humans have fought. This is an invisible force, where there is no symptom nor indication, yet she is very contagious as she is very convincing. I know we the citizens of this one world must tackle this issue like an emergency and quarantine all from getting this virus.

As she but spreads, she becomes stronger and the only way she spreads is by hunting down an innocent soul whom she can prey on. We must stop her by blocking her at her birth. We can only win if we unitedly hold hands and become one human race. I had written about this issue within my blog posts and I know it is still not enough for me, a citizen of this world, to tackle this beast on my own.

She has a huge vehicle which she drives, but she breaks all the rules. I have a small vehicle and I drive only within the laws of the land. My vehicle is not even noticeable by all the big vehicles with name plates upon them. My words are like whispers within the wind and they get lost within the brewing storms of the wrong.

This huge vehicle has placed barricades all around, taking humans astray. I know I must get a huge vehicle to help me or give me a ride to unite all the big vehicles to break the barricades placed by this wrong vehicle. I watch each day, more and more innocent victims fall prey to this monster.

On one hand, she is attacking innocent people. With the other hand, she is creating more monsters as the victims are waking up with only revenge within their mind, body, and soul. I watch the victory dance of the monsters as now they blame the victims as perpetrators.

A monster buried within one's inner soul is but one's biggest enemy, for now this invisible monster shall awaken and wipe out all within her path, even you her creator. From Heavens above, I have been blessed with a dream in which I was in a vehicle of a world leader who had put one hand out through the window and as he drove his vehicle, he was pushing away all of the barricades placed by this monster. He asked me to open my window and place one of my hands out through the window, so unitedly we can work to resolve this problem that but contaminates the world. I asked him, "But how do I even accomplish this?" He told me, "Have faith and it shall be."

I gathered all my faith as I started my work through the only things I have, my pen and paper. Words of the wise have but guided us throughout eternity, so maybe today my sacred words from my inner soul of love will but awaken the world leaders to my call. Complete faith I have within all the world leaders, as I have seen miracles happen through my blessed dreams.

I know there is a reason I have been shown these blessed dreams. Even when there was no hope, like the glowing candles within a dark room, hope had appeared within my life. I hold on to the sweet prayers I but call songs, as my first step to unite all race, color, and religion was to publish my prayer books for all whom but seek hope.

Today, however, I know I must take pen to paper and write about my innermost beliefs and thoughts. I believe at this stage, the world needs a person who can take on a beastly monster that but brews within the contaminated humans. As

I searched all over this Earth for one such person, again in my dream, I found myself sharing a stage with a world leader who was also worried as to how we can vaccinate the world population from being contaminated by this catastrophic virus.

He is a sacred person who within my dreams was shown as a very spiritual being. I walked with him as The Holy Archangels showed me within this sacred soul are the teachings of his father and grandfather. I saw an orange tree had been planted within a land. The original person who had planted this tree walked with me as he showed me this land and her children had amongst them a teacher who can help. I knew the land owner was Alex. Within my dream, I knew this land is the home of the Peace Palace.

A few years later, I was in the New Church in Delft, standing in front of William the Silent. I admire world leaders and their left behind path of victories and failures which but guide us upon our path. As I stood there, I shed tears for a person whose path never met my path. Yet, I felt a strange connection as I remembered walking with him like a miracle within my dreams. I prayed for him and his nation as I promised if there is anything I the owner of a small vehicle could do, then I would do so.

Within this land, people from different parts of the world arrive to find peace and justice. For peace and justice, today I ask all the world leaders and you the individual citizen, please awaken yourselves to this apocalypse we but have upon our hands. Please take on this subject as within your hands, oh the great leaders of this world, lays the future of all people seeking equality within all ethnicity, race, color, religion, gender identity, and sexual orientation as their birthright. We know we need the blessings of the beyond to tackle this problem. We have upon us, this world and her sacred leaders who can in union fight this battle of hate crimes.

The world has now taken herself within the shelters of the world leaders to save herself from the destructions of the instigators of the hate crimes. You the instigator, the owner of self-inflicted injured souls, enter through the back door and hunt your prey until you but convert them into your replicas. We need to get all of you the culprits of the dark nights out into the open air and place a reflecting mirror in front of you, so you the judge but now can judge yourself through your life lived.

The world now has the statistics of a nightmare brewing as the perpetrators of these crimes are undercover.

Even though the world can no longer hide what has been hidden for thousands of years, the differences between the humans have become an overnight calamity, created by the perpetrators of the overnight crimes. Land after land has started to record the rising sea levels.

At the same time, we also see the rise of the inner monsters within human souls. The mighty and powerful sharks of the unjust sea attack the innocent for just being different. I call this, the apocalyptic times as the wise had but warned us of this apocalypse from the past. I call her *The World Hate Crisis*.

I hope and pray the world leaders know how to take over and somehow unitedly with the citizens resolve this problem. I know if anyone can, then this land I visited twice within my life thus far, where the Peace Palace stands tall, will be able to guide. So, within this book, I call upon all the blessed leaders of this world to come stand in front of the Peace Palace. Spread hope within yourself, within your country, and all whom but follow you.

I ask all of the leaders to light a candle in your hands in front of the Peace Palace. Take the oath to awaken this world to be a better and safer place for all humans with humanity. The world leaders, please walk with a glowing candle in your hands throughout the dark nights to bring hope and blessings upon all the homes throughout this world.

Please take over this issue and leave your footprints for all to see how unitedly we can resolve this catastrophe that is brewing all over this world. May the Peace Palace glowing behind and the sacred leaders carrying a candle within their hands, be our picture of peace and our protection from this catastrophic beast. Within my dream, I promised the leader William the Silent, that I, a citizen of this world, will do my share to bring peace upon this Earth.

So, I call upon all of the sacred world leaders to participate in this event and be the candles of hope, for this world. Blessed be the world leaders who can unitedly end even *The World Hate Crisis*. All the protection agencies agree that this is a huge storm brewing amongst us. Within the United States, the Hate Crime Statistics Act was passed by Congress, as ACT 28 U.S.C. § 534 in 1990. Within Europe, the European Court of Human Rights also has very strict rules to hold the perpetrators of these hate crimes accountable as hate crimes are not to be tolerated.

Basic human rights give us humans the right to live our life our way as long as we abide by the laws of the land. I wonder why do we still not have enough data on hate crimes where a victim is only targeted for being different? Innocent victims are being targeted for their perspective, race, gender, religion, ethnicity, sexual orientation, or for having a disability.

Today, I ask you the citizen to awaken and not walk away blindly from these victims. They cannot talk for themselves, but you can. When a person is being targeted for being different, what does the victim say, or who does the victim ask for help?

When a child asks you, "Why are you beating me up?" What would you the perpetrator say? "Because your skin color is different," or "Because the religion you were born into conflicts with mine," or "Because you are just different."

Tears fall throughout the Earth from Heavens above as the skies open up watching injustice. I ask you the human, does your inner soul not once but clench for these innocent souls who are victimized for being just perfect? They are not different. It is you the perpetrators who are but different. You are the beast this world fights. You shall find within the mirror in front of you, the evil you fear the most, your hatred toward all others.

I ask all the world leaders, religious scholars, and scientific scholars to unite at this time against this invisible evil that we all must fight. It is now we must save the human population from this invisible disease that but spreads throughout time. Remember we all have limited time upon this world, yet this hate crisis has no time limit as this evil force is invisible and travels throughout time.

Stop this force now as we the mortals unite and fight the immortal force of evil by awakening all humans with humanity. Remember, hatred but grows from within your inner fears as you are absolutely scared of the situation. It is not your victims but you the perpetrators who are your own victims of your inner hatred. This disease you suffer from has no sympathy for you alone have created this monster. It is you who alone shall suffer for it is only a matter of time, you the creator of all hate crimes shall be exposed.

Peace shall always prevail as we the humans awaken with humanity. We shall be guided by the greatest guides throughout history, also known to all as the politicians, the philosophers, the teachers, the humans with humanity. The historical figure, Kofi Annan had said while accepting the Nobel Peace Prize, "We need to think of the future and the planet we are going to leave to our children and their children" ("The Nobel Peace Prize"). We the humans only need to unite and be guided by our inner selves, for the future generations.

The path created by the past is there to guide all throughout time, but it is always the individual who must walk upon the path placing only his or her own footsteps.

CHAPTER TWO

TOUR GUIDES OF THIS WORLD

"Throughout the dark stormy nights, guiding us the lost and confused, are but the tour guides of this world."

-Ann Marie Ruby

We the humans are always seeking guides to be guided by as we find our temporary housing upon Earth. Yet, I am always being guided from beyond by my Lord, my Creator. Within the footsteps of international citizens, we can build a house upon the chest of Mother Earth. When the house is complete, it will accommodate all the children of Mother Earth with a strong moral foundation. Footprints left in the sand by travelers need a leader who can guide all to their destinations.

While walking on the Scheveningen beach in the Netherlands, I watched my footprints upon the sand had erased as people walked behind me. I know if a world leader had walked, then the path would have converted to a separate road for all to travel throughout time. The footprints of a leader would remain in the pages of history. The footprints of a stranger like me would go unnoticed like the author whose words you know, but the name would not be known to the future.

I pray for the pure soul of a world leader to join me in this fight of mine. Vacations are a period of time we the humans but wait for. Where does your soul travel to, as you dream about this period for days? For my spiritual soul though, I have learned to vacation even within my own home. As I meditate to remove all the worldly obstacles from my mind, body, and soul, I have my personal vacation. No money is spent, and no time is taken away from anyone.

I still end up taking a vacation from everything even on a vacation. It always brings the true perspective of my life back to me. Always within my inner soul, I escape to the reality of my existence. The devotion of my life is for all humans to awaken with humanity.

I have been blessed to be able to travel throughout this world as I have learned to save every dime and realized I could travel and live a simple life. Through my journeys, however, I realized how uniquely similar we the humans are. How do we the citizens adapt to the ever-changing world and the population?

With migration, we have again upon us a huge problem within our hands. Respect and give your guests time and space, we are taught. As guests, you are taught to respect and honor your host. What happens when you but migrate to another country? Are you then a guest or are you then the adopted child of your adopted motherland?

I had a blessed experience when I walked into McDonald's in India. McDonald's does not serve any beef or pork to respect and incorporate the culture and different religious views of India within its menu. In Australia and the European countries, the menu differs as it is made to suit the culture and taste buds of the locals. Always keeping the original menu as similar as it is able to, McDonald's tries to add variety to please the local people while respecting local cultures.

I felt proud as an American to see how McDonald's had thought about the citizens of this world. The American fast food restaurant honors all different race, color, and religion with its international menus. I wondered if McDonald's can travel to different countries and respect different cultures while keeping its own dignity, then how could we the humans but forget?

A person traveling to Europe should respect the culture within the land he or she but enters. This rule applies for all the travelers who are traveling throughout this world. Respect other cultures and always abide by the laws of the land. Respecting other cultures does not make you a racist, but a person who is willing to adapt to your adopted country and take with you love and respect as you add to your adopted motherland your own heritage.

This fast food giant had adjusted its menu to satisfy all the inhabitants of the countries it has been blessed to be within. When you travel to another land or even migrate, you must adapt to the law of the land. It is then you shall find peace as she is your adopted mother.

We the citizens must accept our different siblings into our one home in peace. As they adapt, we too must adapt and blend in harmony together. It is like having a platter of international cuisine. We blend all of the international cuisine on our dinner table as we break bread in union. The smell and taste of freshly baked bread being broken by different colored hands is a sight I would love to have in my home around my dinner table.

I believe just like food, we are all the same, yet different because of our own cultures and upbringing. I have firsthand experiences as I have traveled and seen we the humans share the same feelings and teardrops. While sitting in a foreign movie theater, I watched people share the tears as we were all enjoying a very sad movie in union. We laughed and cried together. As everyone walked out into the daylight, however, I watched each individual to be very restricted within his or her own created walls.

Different race, color, and religion had united to see a movie we all loved, but later it was like no one cared for each other's feelings. What had just happened? Was it because the lights were turned off and we could not see each other, so we accepted all equally? The daylight dawned upon all and again the separation of feelings was very visible. I wondered what I could alone do in this situation.

I know I have to do something to unite all humans within the daylight. Fearful of the dark we the humans are, yet why is it we are afraid to show our true feelings within the daylight? I asked myself as I stood in front of the Peace Palace, how could we unite all race, color, and religion, without violating each person's personal belief or freedom?

As I watched a huge group of spiritual leaders and devotees walking into the Peace Palace, I knew we still had hope. I felt this unusual feeling of peace and harmony as I just stood watching the Peace Palace. I had visited the Netherlands twice and, on each occasion, the Peace Palace was closed to the public as they had private events going on.

I had tied a ribbon on the Wishing Tree and prayed for world peace. As I tied a ribbon for peace, I watched so many people from all around the globe had also come to tie a ribbon on the Wishing Tree. I watched in peace as I believe a country will never fail if differences are included and converted into a tree where all take shelter for peace. I watched the Peace Palace and knew this was my hope for peace.

The International Court of Justice is a place all sacred souls should go and visit if they can afford to do so. I realized I was there for a reason as I know I must knock upon all doors to find the human who but can help unite all humans with humanity. I prayed all humans receive the guidance to be united within humanity. I prayed for this world to be eradicated of the growing hate crisis.

All throughout my trip, I felt someone was watching out for me or was guiding me, as I saw the statues of William the Silent standing tall and watching over all of the citizens of his beloved land. As I sat praying, I realized this world had begun to spill over the brink, as hate messages were the waves overflowing from the oceans to the lands and crossing all borders. When a powerful voice of division throws a word of hate into the air, these hateful words take life, and begin to spread faster than even wildfires.

When natural or unnatural wildfires spread, like they did in 2018 within British Columbia, Canada, and within the states of Washington and California, we the inhabitants of greater Seattle in Washington State experienced the worst air pollution ever. The smoke, like an unnatural fog, had covered the sky. The air quality had dropped as the smoke spread to Seattle from Canada. This smoke felt like a choke holder on our physical bodies.

I personally felt the chest pain and wondered what was going on, until all of my neighbors told me they too felt the same symptoms. I wondered why I was being affected by a wildfire that was not even within my vision. I could not see the land, or hear the citizens, or even share their personal loss of property, but I too had personally suffered from this unwanted and unseen event.

Like the unwanted smokes from a land far away from my own home had touched my physical body, the hateful words of the perpetrators of the hate crimes touch my inner soul as they spread worldwide. The tears of the victim touch my mind, body, and soul as these teardrops make a permanent house within all of the sacred citizens globally.

Life is an example from nature. The effects of even words but spread all over this world and get situated within history throughout time. As I walked near the Peace Palace, I wondered how *The World Hate Crisis* has been spreading worldwide. We can see and try to stop or even prevent the wildfires with care and caution. How do we stop *The World*

Hate Crisis? She is an invisible force stronger than water, fire, air, or even Earth herself.

I had visited Brussels, Belgium during one of my trips. As I stood in front of the Cathedral of St. Michael and St. Gudula, I watched people from all different faiths walk inside and light a candle in hope for blessings to befall upon them. As I walked in, I heard a choir singing "Ave Maria."

Tears again found their way out of my stubborn eyes and my emotions failed in front of all. I again prayed for all of the humans, yes forgetting my own wounds and my own obstacles of life. I know I tried to be selfish as I thought, but I have so many problems looming all around me. Why is it I cannot even pray for myself? Am I selfish when I, a human, think why waste a prayer when this world is in danger from this invisible force which they but see not? What could I do? Why does my heart cry for all the unknown citizens of this world?

In front of me, a small child ran whose parents were lighting a candle. The child said in a loud voice, "But why are you lighting up a candle if you just said you do not believe in this religion?" I did not know what to say or do as I knew this child would grow up with only what is being taught to her. I hoped her parents would also teach her to respect one another even if you are different.

I walked out of the Cathedral and watched all the European Union leaders and their vehicles were going around as they had some kind of gathering at their headquarters. All different race and color walked in union as they hugged and left for their individual countries. During my trip back to the Netherlands from Belgium, I knew there was a reason I had seen this amazing vision of unity amongst the world leaders.

How is it they can keep their differences aside and work in union for the sake of this one world? I remembered peace and the Peace Palace. I thought of how throughout time, we have great humans who but take birth to only awaken the human population from their sleep.

As darkness came upon us when our tour group returned back within the Netherlands, I had an uneasy feeling as I thought something was missing. I wondered what my soul was seeking. I saw in the news how hate crimes have but spread throughout the United States. Somehow people are waking up to the differences amongst themselves. I only wished humans would unite for their similarities.

One night, I heard a gentleman's voice I had never met, but I had seen him within my dreams so many times that I knew him very well. In my dream, he had introduced himself as Izzak. Within my dream was another handsome man who introduced himself as Hans. They asked me if I could send someone the message, "Work for each other, not against each other." I did not know who this person was, but I assumed him to be a world leader.

When I woke up, I sent this message to all of whom I could, who I thought needed this message. Throughout the wheels of time, however, I forgot about these people as life is but a wagon where even the messages given during the daylight hours but fade away. The messages from dreams but take their own time to reveal themselves at the right time and place.

On my way back to The Hague from Belgium, I had seen the refugees trying to camp out in Brussels. I knew the living conditions were very hard. I thought of the citizens of Brussels having mixed emotions as they have given food and shelter to people who appreciate at times. Yet amongst them, some of the refugees are attacking the host country, they but take shelter within.

What is a citizen to do? Trust one's inner feelings of humans with humanity? Or a parent's nightmare, what if one of these people but becomes an attacker? We have landed upon a time zone where trust, honor, dignity, and courage have become the victim of the fearful minds.

My trip throughout the Netherlands had been very peaceful and filled with amazing memories of new places and newly found friends. It felt weird as my trip was coming to an end. Tired and lost within my own self, I had been walking in the dark as I almost slipped off of a curb. A very strong hand held me as he only uttered the sound "Ah!" I saw him and said, "Mark?" He said in Dutch, "Ja, ja, ja (yes)."

I told him, "I am Ann Marie." At that moment, he spoke in very clear English as he told me to walk carefully as these roads are uneven. It was a very small encounter as we went our separate paths. I kept the memory of that moment within my soul. I could not believe he is a prime minister who walks amongst the people, who but rides his bicycle, and wipes off coffee spilled by himself.

I had been to a bookstore earlier to buy some books. One of the employees told me all of the politicians are fake. They do all of this for publicity. This comment of hers had placed a big burden within my inner soul as I was but searching for a soul who would do whatever it takes to awaken humanity.

I sought the soul who would help awaken the citizens' faith within their politicians. Maybe this person knows how he or she can bottle up some love, honor, and justice for all the future generations to open as they but awaken to a newly found world. This bottle will be their blessing as the world would have eradicated *The World Hate Crisis*.

My personal encounter with a complete stranger, however, united my personal faith with my dreams. The positive vibes have replayed the amazing words from people I had never met before. I thought of my own words, "Dreams are blessings from within the soul. Make them into reality as you travel through the journey of life." My inner spirit guided me to this amazing leader who had for the sake of humanity held on to me, so I do not fall.

I know he will hold on to all if he only could fit all within his hands. The path is there, and it may be hard and far away, yet I know faith is believing, not questioning. So, I believe Mark Rutte is the leader who brought my faith back in all the world leaders. I believe if all the world leaders even had a little bit of humanity within them, then this world will have smiling skies above them, even if not today, maybe tomorrow.

The land where the Peace Palace but stands tall to show this world still has hope, I believe, will start another journey to eradicate *The World Hate Crisis*. I call upon the United Nations and all international organizations to awaken to my call and allow this peaceful process to begin. Let us in union begin the process to once and for all eradicate this crisis. It shall grow faster than all the crises this world but has, for this crisis is brewing within the human mind, body, and soul. Let us in union start somewhere and acknowledge this crisis first for then we shall be able to deal with it.

Like the tour guide who had taken us around Brussels and brought us back to the Netherlands safely, I know the world leaders in union shall be our guide through this crisis as they in union bring us back to safety. So, I call upon the humanity within the souls of these world leaders to hold my hands and take over this tour bus.

I make a wish within the wishing wells of your hands, oh the leaders of this world. Please bless this wish as you accept this challenge. Awaken yourselves within love and blessings of the human race as you walk to eradicate *The*

World Hate Crisis. I know in union, not alone, you can prevent this wildfire from spreading. For the love of our one Earth, you shall eradicate *The World Hate Crisis*.

I seek the footsteps of sacred souls I but call world leaders to guide us out of *The World Hate Crisis*. I know my dreams are just not dreams, but within the near future, they shall be reality. Blessed footsteps of the blessed leaders are but are our guides out of this crisis.

World leaders, the politicians, are also the sacred teachers of this society. They shall guide all, like guiding a classroom of children to graduate. This is why the politicians are also known as the tour guides of this world.

CHAPTER THREE

POLITICIANS THROUGHOUT HISTORY

"Oh the philosophical, the religious, and the scientific scholars, are you too but not politicians from within your own time zone? Have you too left behind footsteps to but unite or divide, with or without your knowledge?"

-Ann Marie Ruby

History teaches us the truth of yesteryears, yet a seer sees the truth of the beyond. What is a politician? A leader chosen by us the citizens. What is a seer? A person who wants to guide us the citizens and our sacred politicians, or a student who wishes to learn from this world and beyond.

Throughout my life, I have always been a student. I believe there is no end to knowledge. Each dawn through dusk through yet another dawn, I acquire so many teachers through the path and the footsteps I travel in life. Today, my thirsty soul searches for a sacred teacher who will guide not only this student but all humans as he or she too becomes a student first, and then a teacher.

I search for a teacher, a politician, and a leader throughout this world. Following the footsteps of past teachers, I realize politicians are born to guide us throughout eternity. Political philosophers were throughout time the greatest gifts for the western civilization. When and where we had a great civilization, we had philosophers guide society through the most difficult times.

We have at this moment within history, arrived upon yet another time zone where we need another great philosopher, a teacher, a human with humanity, to guide us. Some might argue, however, that without realizing at times, the philosophers too have divided amongst us the humans. It is then we the humans must learn to disagree and agree upon this note like a teacher who stands in the classroom and listens to both sides of constructive criticism. Or, like a politician who sits within the parliament and listens to all different groups, but can walk away smiling for peace and justice in this world.

Plato, one of the greatest European philosophers, was born in Athens, Greece. In addition to being a philosopher, he was a political leader and the founder of the first higher learning institution which led to European universities and western philosophy. His impact on this world is still felt today. Plato believed within a society, it is normal to not agree on every aspect of life, which makes a balanced society. Additionally, the Greek civilization made way for the western idea of democracy.

Politicians who smile and accept all different opinions can still be your friend looking out for your best interest. At times, we may or may not agree with all of their viewpoints, and we can openly tell them our objections. In this balanced society, these politicians would accept our views and walk with us, for us, in union.

Aside from the Western European philosophers, there were other great philosophers worldwide, such as the Chinese philosophers Confucius and Sun Tzu, and the Indian philosophers Adi Shankara and Sri Bhagavad Ramanujacharya. This world should not exclude any philosophers but should include all from around this globe.

This world is like a school with different classes and different teachers with different topics. This is how the great scholars became known and have left behind their footprints. Learn and walk with your eyes open. Philosophers like Plato and his messages to this day, are left behind with us as we travel through life. We are still being guided by the philosophers of the past because they too, I believe, were politicians.

Plato had said in *The Republic*, "The human race will have no respite from evils until those who are really philosophers acquire political power or until, through some divine dispensation, those who rule and have political authority in the cities become real philosophers" ("Plato").

I ask all of you, is it not possible to have amongst us another philosopher, a politician, who can guide us through the present time? Where our views would be different, but we could agree to disagree? Where the obstacles of the past, present, and future would be talked about from different perspectives of different beholders? It is time we search for a leader, a teacher, a human with humanity to but guide all.

Mahatma Gandhi said in *An Autobiography: The Story of My Experiments with Truth*, "It is now my opinion that in all Indian curricula of higher education there should be a place for Hindi, Samskrit[1], Persian, Arabic, and English, besides of course the vernacular" (18). The great leader wanted his citizens to learn not just his or her own language and culture, but a little from all around this Earth. He must have known the Indian population would travel all around to be citizens of this Earth, not just of India.

Do I agree with all the philosophers and the political figures of the past and present? I would say yes and no. I respect them. I also listen to them, but I walk with my own feet, not theirs. Is it not but them who have taught us to agree, and to disagree? I want to build a society where we can walk hand in hand, and agree to disagree. I want to have a society where we can live in peace and harmony.

I admire the Nobel Laureate, Rabindranath Tagore, who said in *Personality*, "The highest education is that

---

[1] Alternate spelling of the word "Sanskrit" quoted directly from M.K. Gandhi's *An Autobiography: The Story of My Experiments With Truth*

which does not merely give us information but makes our life in harmony with all existence" (116). I search for the philosophers, the religious scholars, and the scientists who but walk for all in union. Where division is but seen as the biggest obstacle of life, I search for the wise, the just, and the honorable. I search for a human with humanity.

Pope Francis said in a message at the end of Ramadan in 2013, "Regarding the education of Muslim and Christian youth, we have to bring up our young people to think and speak respectfully of other religions and their followers, and to avoid ridiculing or denigrating their convictions and practices."

Memories of 9/11 still haunt me. After 9/11, the world had divided and given in to fear. What do we do when we are afraid to say anything, for or against a view? Brewing inner feelings could cook up a catastrophe beyond human comprehension.

I had watched a Muslim family walk in tears in Maryland as they watched the Sandy Hook Elementary School shooting on the television. They wanted to lend a helping hand, but they were too scared to even share their feelings. I asked a stranger why this feeling was bothering her. She told me, "The first prayer is let everyone be safe," but as a Muslim, she could not help but think, "Let this not be another Muslim terrorist attack." When the identity of the perpetrator comes to view, it is then they do not know what to do or say. If they go to show their support, people reject them. If they stay away, people criticize them. What are they to do?

Muslim terrorists have done so much damage to this world, including the innocent Muslims who are trying to live a peaceful life. Criminals are nothing but just criminals. Religion is there for you the individual to be guided by, not for you to take away the personal belief and freedom of another. Differences are but a beautiful rainbow of colors. Stand up for each other and become the rainbow across this globe.

I again believe this is only possible if we but have a philosopher, a politician, a teacher, and a human with humanity. We need a teacher who can take all of these universal problems upon his or her shoulders. The solution but lays within the hands of a united group that walks for you, and with you. Even when they disagree, it is because they watch over the society as a whole. We need a person who is willing to light the candles of hope within all houses.

Mother Teresa had said, "If I ever become a saint—I will surely be one of 'darkness.' I will continually be absent from Heaven—to light the light of those in darkness on earth" (Mother Teresa and Kolodiejchuk 1). This is what I have been talking about. We need people like Mother Teresa back on Earth to lead us through these dark times. I had written a prayer for all in hope maybe as we unite, we can be the candles of hope throughout this universe for all.

I ask all the world leaders to be our candles of hope, as you walk with a candle in your hands for all humans. This Earth has chosen you to be our leader, so you can keep her children safe. Hold on to the child next to you even though he or she might be different from you. Show all you love the child, just as you love your inner soul.

For me, I love all the children of this Earth. If I could, I would adopt all the children of this Earth, so there would be no orphan. There would be no more perpetrators of hate crimes, for between the crime and the criminal my child would face, I the mother but would stand. Today, for all my inspiration upon you, I give you my written prayer. Oh the world leaders, may you be an inspiration for one and all as you become the inspiration of hope and blessings.

CANDLES OF HOPE

My Lord,

With the sun setting in Your vast sky,

The Earth but is in the dark.

May I, Your devotee,

Be there with a candle in my hand.

My Lord,

As the night sky but turns dark with

Your moon trying to peek through to give us hope,

May I, Your devotee,

Be there with a candle in my hand.

My Lord,

As house after house

But turns dark, searching for light,

May I, Your devotee, be the light bearer

With a candle in my hand.

My Lord,

As Your moon and twinkling stars

Try to send the message of Your sun's birth,

As all but watch out for the birth of Your sun,

May we, the creation,

Await and light up each house one by one

As we carry

The

CANDLES OF HOPE.

May we in union be able to overcome this obstacle and get rid of *The World Hate Crisis*. Science has also come on board as it has now come along the path of positive thinking. According to various scientific facts, we can heal ourselves with positive thinking. Like the sunny day gives us rays of hope, a dull and cloudy day but pours the negative energies within the mind, body, and soul. Scientific evidence has supported raising a child in a positive environment will but help the child grow up to be a positive and energetic person.

It is we the humans who need to guide ourselves out of this unnatural calamity that but waits to attack us. We need to find the human or the group that can unite and agree to disagree for the sake of humanity. I know we are but alone and lost within this dark stormy night, floating all around.

Instead of helping each other, we are but drowning one another. At this stage, we the humans must call upon our inner humanity and like the philosophers, the religious scholars, or the scientific scholars, we too must listen to the wise. Awaken the inner wisdom within your inner soul. I call upon all whom can stand up in union to guide us through this stormy night. Let us in union awaken to fight *The World Hate Crisis*.

Within each house, we must light a candle to keep the glowing hope going. Through the neighborhoods, all the houses shall but glow. In union, we the humans will be the candles of hope for all the teardrops of the lost and stranded souls who but ask, seek, and knock for just one blessed sign of hope.

The great philosophers, the Nobel Laureates, the religious saints, and other historical figures from the United States, through the European continent, and throughout this Earth, have all tried to create a better and safer place for us to but live within. Some we agree with, and some we do not. We have now landed upon a time when politicians, philosophers, religious scholars, and even scientific scholars are having a hard time to guide us or to agree amongst themselves. The difference of opinions that has barricaded an individual or a group from society is but greater than what anyone could have predicted.

As I had gone through the footsteps of the past, I asked myself, where do we go from here? I know we must unite. We must choose to respect our differences and let our differences be our guide to our union. Respect all as they too are but different just like you. It is you, the different, who must awaken for all and unite all on this day. I believe we need a teacher, a politician, a scholar who but loves differences and holds on to the hands of all different people within one house.

Finding someone who can lead this cause for all humans to unite is so difficult. It is the person or the people who but carry this same feeling, who then must step up and volunteer. I had walked into the New Church in Delft where I saw William the Silent still waits to be resurrected. There is Latin writing which translates to, "Here lies William I, Father of the Fatherland, awaiting the Resurrection."

I have a family member who had climbed the 376 steps of the New Church, in the second highest tower of the Netherlands. The tower itself is around 357 feet, or 108.75 meters, in height. He had joined our group later on our Delft tour as he screamed and told all, "It is your dream of William and the orange tree!"

I watched him and he knew I was upset at him for saying this aloud. Yes, I had dreams guiding me through the Netherlands, where there was a William, who I knew was asleep and who was linked to an orange tree. I never knew where this country was. I kept seeing dreams of the orange tree calling me, until one day I had the dream of Mark Rutte.

That is when I had placed a name to this land that calls me from far away.

I saw different historical figures and the difference of opinions within William the Silent's historical life all around as I remembered walking with him in a dream I had seen. I know this is a historical figure from the past of a country that was unknown to me, yet I had seen him walking with me. I had cried and told him, but I am not from your country, so why do I see you? The answer remains within the future. As I saw the orange tree carpet within his Delft home, I knew that I had seen the same orange tree within my dreams. I had asked, why? There was no answer as I just remained silent.

Who would I choose to lead this crisis that is brewing up a huge storm on our Earth? I cannot call upon the past heroes or the Earth to awaken and give us someone who has proven his or her love for this Earth. I know this crisis shall but pick her leader.

Again my thoughts went to a person within the Netherlands who is a teacher and a politician, and a human with humanity. I know there are so many world leaders who can take on *The World Hate Crisis*. The world leaders can unite and maybe come up with a solution to this situation. I again ask all the world leaders, please volunteer to take upon your hands this crisis and maybe with all the world leaders in union, we will know how to end *The World Hate Crisis*.

I believe, hatred is but buried within the lowest level of the human conscience. There is absolutely no asking and receiving, when a person is harmed in any way by another human. How do you harm what does not belong to you? How do you harm what you can never replace? Hatred toward a person for just being different within my eyes is but the biggest crime within existence. You the perpetrator of these crimes are but going against The One Creator and The Lord's creation.

We the inhabitants of Earth must awaken and call upon all the world leaders to do their share, to end *The World Hate Crisis*. As you but walk ahead and lay your footsteps to guide us, oh the world leaders, please hold on to all of us. Let us be ourselves as you teach us to unite through our differences.

The world will finally find peace through the eradication of hate crimes. For this, we the citizens, but need to accept the different leaders and their different opinions. We need to learn to agree to disagree, and be guided by the politicians throughout history.

CHAPTER FOUR

MIRACLES FROM THE BEYOND

"A human who but awakens to lead all throughout the natural and unnatural calamites is but a leader with miracles from the beyond."

-Ann Marie Ruby

The journey of life is but a complete miracle where obstacles and blessings come without knocking. Some of us are blessed as we knock upon the doors of miracles. As the miracles come and let us know what the future is, they leave their sacred messages within the past. These miracles then knock upon the doors of blessed travelers to become the blessed miracles.

The invisible path is only visible through the footprints of a sacred traveler who journeys to guide one and all. Setting up a map through the footprints as you guide all through your political careers, you are but the miracle from beyond that our united souls seek. Throughout the lands, all around this Earth, there is unrest, mistrust, and dishonesty.

I had traveled from Florida to Washington State in my recreational vehicle on a cross country vacation. I felt like I had embarked upon a blessed journey. For the first time though, I was scared of driving.

What if I get stopped for no reason? What if someone comes and attacks my vehicle? What if there is gang violence and I get stuck in between?

I had stopped for gas and found a heavy argument over the recent election and mistrust. I saw the anger and resentment had grown within all race. I saw mistrust amongst race, color, and religion. I saw division within the eyes of the different. Never did I see or feel any differences or any hate crisis brewing around all the houses, but I saw this environment develop for the first time. What did I do?

Well, like a coward or you could say a smart person, I left on my own way, pretending not to hear. Was I right or wrong? I do not know, but I wanted to keep myself and the people who traveled with me safe first.

We all tried to look up the local news to see if anything had happened, but there was no news. The gas station was intact the next day and all seemed exactly the same as the night before. I prayed it was just a fair argument and nothing more.

This mistrust did not stop within the United States. As I had traveled overseas, I witnessed the same feelings. Humans had mistrust, fear, and a deep hidden anger brewing within their souls.

I saw the fear of terrorist attacks was even within my soul as I had kept an eye on the people all around me. I told myself I was just keeping an eye out for anything suspicious. It was my duty to do so.

I made myself understand, yet I was scared and thought it is not fair for anyone to be scared. There are those who are scared of the terrorists, and those who are innocent but being observed and kept under an eye even though they are innocent. I know how you feel for being questioned even though you are innocent. What do you and I do?

Let us eradicate the problems from our own homes first. Let us the parents turn our own children in if we think they are the criminals we are all but afraid of and for whom innocent people are being harassed. I believe all the children of this Earth are but ours and we are but the parents of all children. For the sake of all the children, awaken oh the parents as The Creator has but chosen you to bring up your children. If and when they have wronged, then it is your first right as a creation of The One Creator to take that child to the authorities.

What do I but do to end *The World Hate Crisis* and how am I being fair to all? I asked myself, what is the right thing to do? Why does this bother me?

What are the innocent people, the victims who have been affected, and the innocent lives that will never return, to do? What about the families of the victims? Is there anyone on this Earth who can hold these people and bring peace back within their souls?

Religious and racial wars had begun before our time, and with knowledge and education, we thought this kind of unjust war had but stopped. Why is it we are now going backward? Instead of going forward, why are we walking toward a catastrophe?

Hate crimes appear within the air like flying arrows as the voices of the wrongful humans are much more harmful than the natural breeze. People are being attacked in buses and trains, yet no one stands up to say anything against these horrible crimes. I watch all the news networks reporting these crimes, but people who are standing around say nothing and just walk away.

I watched a horrific event as a person was beaten up for being different, yet all the passengers remained quiet. Someone had secretly recorded this event but was afraid to openly object. As I watched this event replay on the television, I started to cry for the innocent person being beaten up only because the person was of a different faith. What has happened to the humans who were brought up with basic moral values? Where are the warriors with faith, honor, and justice?

When a human stands alone for being born different or does not identify him or herself within any gender, race, color, or religion, what is his or her fault? Hate crimes based on gender identity and sexual orientation are but crimes where the innocent soul of the victim is harmed by the wrongful mighty humans who think they were born perfect. I wanted to shout and tell all to leave the children of The Creator alone for they too are but the creation.

I had personally been attacked as I chose to live a celibate life. I chose to be abstinent from any sexual activities as I want to wait for my husband to come and enter my life. Just like the victims of gender and sexual orientation hate crimes, I felt victimized for being celibate.

I wondered who the sinner was. The innocent? Or the criminals who think themselves beyond any judgment for they become the judge?

This sentiment is being felt throughout schools, universities, workplaces, and everywhere a person chooses to be celibate. Where have we landed? Why can we not accept personal choices of individual beings and let everyone choose his or her path as long as it is within the laws of the land? Why is it either your way or no way? The power of your hate crimes has the lands burning and spreading ashes, touching all humans across this globe.

My soul had cried for the unknown souls whom I had but bumped into during my two-year stay within downtown Seattle. Downtown Seattle was beautiful and peaceful, yet I had left my apartment and bought a single-family house because of human pressure and criticism from the harsh voices of society I could not take. I loved being downtown and that everything was within walking distance.

I do not like driving at all. My apartment life, however, became a nightmare as all the eyes of the strangers had wondered why I had chosen to be single. They questioned what was wrong with me. I wondered why they would ask that.

As a spiritual person who has taken the vow of celibacy, I never gave a thought to their behaviors except when it became annoying in the elevators. I had fibbed for the first time and told everyone I was betrothed.

I wish I had the courage to tell all that I live within the commandments of my Lord. I could not understand why my personal choice to be single bothered anyone. I had watched single women, single divorced women, and single women with children were attacked for not having a man by their side. I never realized how big this issue was until I lived in an apartment where we had all of the above.

One day as I was crying, I tried to go to my apartment after again being harassed by spoiled women who held on to their men possessively. They would ask over and over if I had my man yet? For them, I continued to fib and say oh he lives abroad. I had felt the pressure to do so as I did not want anyone forcing me on a date.

As I had stepped into the lobby one day, I saw a full-fledged argument had broken out of control. I wanted to go back to my apartment and not be involved in any of these arguments, yet I had spoken out. Not for myself did I speak as I could take on my own pain, but the pain of others bothered me.

I wondered what was going on as I saw the same women were arguing with two men who also lived in the same apartment building. The two men were engaged and were celebrating their union as a gay couple. All different people had come up and ganged against this couple. I asked all, "How are you The Judge?" I had congratulated them as I walked past them.

One of the same women teasingly asked if I was like them. I said, "Do not be the voice of a critic who shall be judged!" I wanted to shout and tell all, I am celibate and spiritual by choice and will wait for my soulmate. If I do not find him, then it is alright as I have my Lord. All my love for my Lord and His love for me will be my blessings throughout this journey of my life.

I never said anything as the unjust critics of this world only see what they do as the right path and all that of the others as wrong. I ask you, do not judge the different, be it for gender or sexual orientation, for all humans are but the judged not The Judge. Human beings, awaken to this truth of wisdom and awaken to your inner humanity.

I know every day, the hate crisis is but increasing. I see no relief in view. It is as if all the passengers are lost and stranded within an ocean with no law or guidance to follow.

I had thought people would unite when left within a crisis, but it seems all the people are so scared. They think that to save their own lives, they must go into defense mode. It is how the animals but save themselves.

As the animals are hunted down by the humans, they attack back as their only survival mechanism is but to attack. So, now have we but become the animals or are we but the hunters? The difference between humans and animals is that humans have a blessed gift called the human intelligence.

Where is the relief all spiritual souls are but seeking? I search throughout this world for a path out of this misery. Anger is brewing within all hearts that are but blind and see no reasoning. We the humans have vehicles provided by The Creator, yet some are drunk by choice and therefore cannot control their own vehicles. It is then they see not, and hear not any words from the wise as they are but all intoxicated.

What are we to do at this stage when we the humans have gone astray? We do not see or hear the pain of others. We pretend to ignore and not be responsible for our own actions. I believe we again need Plato, Mahatma Gandhi, or Mother Teresa who can teach us even today from the past. Plato, a wealthy person, was taught by Socrates, the only path to wisdom is by becoming a "lover of wisdom," or basically becoming a philosopher who could lead the nation.

Miracles do happen as even to this day, we the researchers of wisdom search for wisdom. Within miracles, we find wisdom. With the lessons of history, when we find ourselves within a crisis, we can only help ourselves out through the doors of miracles. Miracles are found within the hands of all citizens who but unite for humanity and walk against inhumane treatments of the human race.

A land calls for her leader as she blesses a person to lead the nation. All the world leaders walk for union and harmony within wisdom. With historical lessons as a guide, they can take us out of this situation.

I believe a land filled with miracles and blessings but shall bring upon us a leader. Mother Earth shall awaken a leader who will hold on to the wisdom of the wise, be strong, and with blessings from the Heavens above, shall be there for all humans. This is a job for the united leaders, not just one leader from one nation.

We need someone who can call upon all the nations across this globe and unite all the sacred leaders for one cause, for the love of humanity. I had watched all the world leaders gather in union to discuss the climate crisis, another calamity we the humans must fight. It is then I thought I must ask the world leaders to unite against the invisible crisis of hatred that we but have brewing all across the globe.

I believe miracles from the beyond are the world leaders who unite not for their own name or fame, but for the love of this one world. I believe just as my dreams had guided me to one such human named Mark Rutte, it must be because he, with all world leaders, are but the miracles from the beyond. After my personal interaction with Prime

Minister Mark Rutte, who fights for world climate control, I know we still have hope for all the world leaders like him. They shall all be our hope to victory against *The World Hate Crisis*.

May you the sacred world leaders find within your inner souls, the willpower to awaken to the love and harmony of this one world. You were chosen through democracy by a greater power called love from all the citizens of your land. Find within your mind, body, and soul, the will to stand up in union with all the world leaders and eradicate this crisis now before it becomes the apocalypse of the End of Time.

As you the sacred leaders become a miracle for us, the different and divided, place your blessed hands upon all and guide us to safety with your sacred knowledge. May your guided path be a blessed miracle throughout eternity. Let the visions not be just mine, but of ours, the united citizens of this world, as we convert our visions into reality.

I ask you the world leaders to have the dreams of your citizens within your visions. Today, share their inner tears, their inner love, and inner joy as you make the dreams into reality. Accept all different children as one within your land as they but have chosen you as their hope. May the sacred hands of the sacred leaders but be our guided miracles from the beyond.

CHAPTER FIVE

WEIGHING SCALE

"Why do we the humans but ignore our neighbor's crimes, until they but knock upon our door? Is it not then, the judgment but has been contaminated upon the weighing scale?"

-Ann Marie Ruby

If only we the humans could weigh our action before it takes place, then we would have achieved to avoid so many catastrophes. Yet amongst us, we have miracles through which we are able to see the final result of our action before it even takes place. What are we to do at that stage? Do we keep quiet in fear of being ridiculed?

I would rather be ridiculed than live with regrets. Weighing the humans with anything other than humanity is but against the guidelines of my personal moral values. The knowledge and footsteps were left behind by the religious, philosophical, and scientific scholars of the past to guide all to safety.

Oh the leaders of the past miracles, may the blessed miracles not end but increase through the present and future leaders of this great Earth. Mother Earth has tears falling as she is not able to handle her children's teardrops. The oceans, the rivers, and the lands across this globe are but showing the effects of extreme climate change. We the children of this Earth must do our share to tackle this and take care of our Mother Earth.

The problem, however, is we the children are not united and have but divided amongst ourselves. A mother watches her children fight amongst each other. In the meantime, it is but the mother who suffers. The weighing scale of our bad deeds has overpowered our good deeds and has started to tip and fall upon all the children of this Earth.

Mother Earth now has to protect her children who are being crushed by bad deeds, one of which I call hate crimes. What happens when all of these hate crimes fall upon us? It is then we call this crisis, *The World Hate Crisis*.

I have seen FBI reports regarding hate crimes in the United States. These reports reveal an increase in the number of hate crimes by seventeen percent or so in the past year. Hate crimes have been increasing over the last three years. The statistics are not good globally as hate crimes are spreading like wildfires. The pundits are but saying if the hate crimes increase like this, we will have a catastrophe within our hands. My only worry is like the ignorant neighbors, we will be asleep until the fires but spread to our homes.

What about your children and grandchildren? Do you not want them to grow up hand in hand with their neighbors and feel safe? The sex offenders must be registered to live within any neighborhood for they have a criminal record. What about the people who are but targeting their victims based on race, ethnicity, religion, sexual orientation, gender, ancestry, or for a disability? Hate crime is registered as a crime. Therefore, the perpetrators of hate crimes should also be registered as criminals.

I believe these people should be registered within the pages of history through the pen and paper of the storytellers, as the worst kind of humans in existence. The invisible crime of the corrupt mind, body, and soul, is created by us the society. These humans only spread what but is taught to them.

The teachers of these crimes have lived a safe and peaceful life under the mask of pretense and bigotry. Today, it is but their students who have become even more powerful than the teachers. I wonder if a parent watching his or her child lives with any regret. How does it feel to see your child on the television screen after being exposed for instigating hate crimes?

Do any of these parents feel the shame and low self-esteem of what have they created? I know there are parents who after seeing their own child being exposed as a criminal or creator of hate crimes, have asked the child to leave their homes. There are parents who take their own child to the police themselves.

I know there are citizens around this world who are scared to go to the police in fear of being discriminated against. Driving has become a nightmare. Do you get attacked by a criminal or get attacked by the same police force from whom you but seek protection? Every morning, people try to act normal as they leave for work and say their goodbyes to their families. The hugs given at the doors are big and fearful as there is a cold chill within the air.

I had a personal experience as one of my family members was attacked as he was walking home from work. He was on the phone with me when suddenly I heard his screams. I told him to let go of all of his belongings and run. I started to cry and called upon my Lord as I could not hear anything he was saying. His coworker was walking with him and both of them were screaming until suddenly there was no more noise.

I thought I had a panic attack as all the noises went silent. I received a call from a police officer in a short while. I panicked as his calming voice told me first, "Everything is okay. I want you to talk to someone." I heard my family member and his coworker's calm voices as they told me they were safe.

Luckily there was a police officer on duty going around the block. As he saw these two men were being attacked, he had come to save these two men. He placed himself in between them and the criminal who had escaped. My family member was smart as he had thrown his huge bag and his phone at the criminal who had tried to attack. They screamed loud enough to attract the attention of passersby who also stopped and shouted.

Days have passed and time heals everything, yet this incident stays within my mind as I hear the voices of the phone call haunting me. If a petty thief and his crime knock me out of my soul, I wonder how an unjust hate crime would feel when a brother, a father, or a friend never returns home for being attacked just for being different.

The police officer had been extremely nice and tried to calm down both men as he had dropped them home individually. The blessings of The Lord were upon the young men who were out of high school, trying to earn some money for their families. I wondered what if the criminal had a gun?

Down the memory lane I traveled, as I had been confronted by a person with a gun. I was being followed and honked at for a long time while I was driving on Route 66. I was driving at 70 miles per hour and did not know what was going on. The man following me stopped behind me as I walked into a grocery store. He had two guns on him as he said, "Woman, you drive too slow."

I told him I was driving at the speed limit I thought was safe and within the speed limit allowed by the law. He showed his guns and said he has a lot of guns and no fear. I knew he was an angry man who had his young children with him. They started to cry and told him to calm down. They apologized and told me their father always threatens with a gun. I wanted to call the police but was too scared of a neighbor and his guns.

He told me everyone here drives at 90 miles per hour. I saw he had truth to his words as it seemed like everyone was in a rush. I knew this had touched my inner spirit as I believe in freedom of a person. As long as a person lives within the laws of the land, I have no reason to be scared or afraid of the person. On this occasion, however, I felt violated by this man's action. He had two guns, and a temper which obviously he could not control. He also had young children who were trying to calm him down, but were afraid to voice their fears.

I did not know what to say. Was he a father trying to protect his family for which he carries his guns? Was he a danger to society because he had guns on him? What if his temper betrayed him? Even then, the guns would be in between his temper and an innocent life lost too easily. I had sleepless nights wondering what if I was African American, or Hispanic? Would his reaction have been different? Then, would I have been just a number on a chart that reads, *Victims Lost to Hate Crimes*? I do not know what happened to that family as we went peacefully in our separate ways and had never encountered each other again.

I know gun control is another issue, yet within the hands of a criminal, it is but the weapon of might. Do not give a gun to a child or an animal who has the mental capacity and the mind of judgment less than a child. Hold on to each other as you become the protector of humanity, not the taker of lives.

Asian, Hispanic, black, or white, are all being attacked by one or another. Religious or not, if you are different from your attacker, then you are being attacked. I have read different statistics from worldwide reports which are but all very worrisome. If the number of hate crimes increases at this rate, we will surpass all the catastrophes of this world and shall have within our hands a war the world has not yet but witnessed.

All wars that historically have taken place on this Earth had been between specific groups where you knew who your opponents were. This invisible war is but invisible as it hides within the individual soul of a person, who but walks with you and me. How do we resolve an invisible situation which but attacks from within a person's soul?

How do we end this situation which shall but hunt our future generations throughout time? The first step is to look into the facts of this situation. I have created charts, which I have included in the final chapter of this book, for the recent hate crimes within the United States and around the world. The rate at which hate crimes are increasing is alarming and must be taken into account by all the international organizations.

I also ask all the world leaders not to turn your face to this crisis but take heed of a person who but is just a human with humanity. I search for you, the one who can tackle this situation, as I am but a woman with a small vehicle whose words get lost within the winds like a blessing trying to find the blessed.

What does a single woman do to fight the opposing waves and winds that but keep me from even walking toward them? Who do I trust to hold on to my hands as I but need to stand up against these obstacles of time and tide? How do I know who but is the friend and who but is the enemy? I had always believed true friendship is but the blessed start of a relationship. If you have befriended an enemy of the human society, however, your friend shall take you and all around you down as he or she but sinks.

Remember who you admire or who you follow could be the nightmare of a newly awakened society. My hope is to walk through the pages of history to gain the knowledge of the past lives lived. I know like a lighthouse blinking from beyond, history teaches those of us whom but seek the knowledge. A person guiding from the beyond is but a blessing as we can see the wrong and the right turns of his or her life lived.

I search for a person with moral values who is admired by even the Heavens above and Earth beneath to take charge of this situation. Today, you the sacred person who but awakens to take control over this disaster waiting to happen, will be criticized and ridiculed, but may you awaken beyond all criticism for the sake of all humans who but need you.

May I find at least one world leader willing to take upon his or her shoulders this responsibility. I know my call will but get lost within the ocean of the great and mighty humans. A world leader who has proven him or herself shall be able to call upon all the world leaders to unite for this human cause. I believe this Earth but within her chest has given birth to leaders with humanity who can lead this world to safety.

I believe in the miracles of the beyond as I had visited the magical land of orange and felt an amazing feeling of peace and serenity. William the Silent had restored my faith in the strength of differences. Inclusion of all ethnicities within a group strengthens a society.

It is then we have fingers that are but different. Each finger within a hand is different to give us a stronger grip. The footprints left behind by the sacred leaders of the past are the true blessings this world but needs and seeks to eradicate *The World Hate Crisis*. The future of all humans rests upon the united leaders of this world as they weigh fairly all humans upon their weighing scales.

CHAPTER SIX

HUMANITY BUT AWAKENS

"When calamities but appear from the unknown, it is then we the humans find our inner humanity for each other. Within all apocalyptic crises we see all around us, humanity but awakens."

-Ann Marie Ruby

Humans awaken at dawn as the night's memories are just that, memories. Like the stars blinking upon the night skies, we have blessings fall upon the seers of this world to awaken all humans with humanity. It is then the seers but seek the blessed travelers, who but guide themselves first, then become a leader to guide all thereafter.

The traveler's journey, through the footsteps of the blessed leaders throughout time, is but the only miracle we can weigh to find humanity. I travel through this world as I join in to fight and eradicate world plagues that place our Earth in danger, the one Earth we all call home. The world has even changed her weather pattern as we the inhabitants fight to save our one world.

I admire the world leaders doing their share to fight this catastrophe. I admire the citizens who have but gathered all around this globe to fight this catastrophe in union. I admire the courage of humans who but have been fighting this disaster and are trying to do something to prevent it.

Throughout time, when we but have a common enemy, we the humans unite. We all hold hands and forget all about our personal differences. Not the political leaders nor the religious, philosophical, or scientific scholars can awaken all, but only the individual who is under attack can. Why does it take a knock on your door to awaken yourself?

I thought about my own self. Every morning, the alarm goes off and I press the snooze button until I know I must but awaken. The human population is but asleep, pressing the snooze button for now. I want all of the humans across this globe to awaken now and realize our future is but at risk. We are under attack by our own inner negativities. Our own inner self is what needs to be awakened. For the love of honor and justice, we must remove our inner feelings of us the different and unite for us the human race.

The statistics of the hate crimes are not good and have but taken their own course. The virus is live in the air and we must awaken and do something. I know I have said over and over again to myself, I am only one person. What can I do?

The sun is up outside, and all of the world seems absolutely fine within my part of the Earth. Why should I but care? I care for you the victims of these hate crimes. I want to hold on to you and say, "Please do not think all of the humans have forgotten basic moral values."

We just need to awaken our own self first, then awaken each other. I ask the world to awaken to this catastrophe now. We have the world health crisis and the world food crisis. The world is but incurring all of these crises and new organizations are but taking birth to handle them. Why is it you the leader of a nation, or you the head of an international organization, or you the individual citizen, are not aware of *The World Hate Crisis*? When victims are but shedding tears of injustice, why is it we the humans do not see?

The United Nations walks within different parts of this world to tackle all different crises. I ask you to get involved. The international organizations trying to fund all different projects throughout this world, please get involved. How will all of your efforts to help be helpful if we the humans are but harming each other?

The International Court of Justice, please wipe the tears of a mother who is suffering from hate crimes. A father trying to save his children from being attacked or becoming an attacker himself but needs you too. I call upon all the leaders of this world to awaken and create a new organization which will but handle *The World Hate Crisis*.

Like a wildfire burning everything in her way, this crisis is also burning out of control. It is now when we can still control the situation that we must take over and awaken all of whom are but willing to help. Alone and stranded, I am crying for all humans to awaken with humanity. I know in union, we shall be able to handle all the obstacles this Earth but must handle.

Be this a human made, natural, or unnatural crisis, we the humans in union shall be victorious. All the world leaders can have a united call, where we the humans but shall gather in union to battle all of the obstacles, whatever they may be. I call upon all the world leaders and the individual citizens to volunteer your time and humanitarian services for the sake of humanity. I watch all of you try to solve the problems of your respective land. Today, for the sake of all humans, will you awaken first and call upon your partners throughout this world to unite for humanity?

The current world leaders who are in office or the leaders who have left your service, you have a huge vehicle the humans would but listen to. Place your weight upon this blessed cause and know even if we the present do not see the fruits of this tree that we but plant, the future shall gather around this tree and share her fruits. At that time, it matters not who had planted this tree, but only that the tree had been planted and all of the future are but safe under this tree.

I would like to share a famous quote of the psychologist John B. Watson, who had established the psychological school of behaviorism. He had said,

"Give me a dozen healthy infants, well-formed, and my own specified world to bring them up in and I'll guarantee to take any one at random and train him to become any type of specialist I might select - doctor, lawyer, artist, merchant-chief and, yes, even beggar-man and thief, regardless of his talents, penchants, tendencies, abilities, vocations and the race of his ancestors" (104).

I ask the sacred world leaders to take the responsibility for their respective citizens. With love, honor, and justice, you can take control of your respective houses. See the lost and stranded. Do not divide amongst the children, but unite all with the gentle touch of humanity.

Again, I ask a person who has the love for all creation within your soul, the wisdom of the wise, and the blessed humanity to but awaken yourself first. Then, take upon your shoulders this blessed job. Blessed be the souls of all who but unite to be of service to this world through their sacred footsteps and path. Blessed be the sacred humans who lead on the stage, in front of the open eyes, the opponents, and the supporters, as they but guide through miracles they create for us.

The only goal is to find the sacred humanity within all followers. It is you the leaders who can at this time be of great help to all humans who wait to be rescued as we but face, *The World Hate Crisis*. I believe in humans and I believe we all have within us, humanity. I had an incident that had awakened my faith within humanity.

I was living in downtown Seattle at the time. Downtown Seattle is as diverse as one can imagine. Walking within the crowd makes you feel like you belong there. It matters not what your ethnicity is.

I had come home and was in the lobby of my apartment building, waiting to let in a family member. She called on my cell phone as I asked her why she was delayed. I heard her voice shaken up from something as she started to cry.

I had my dog with me as I started to run toward my family member. I was not thinking straight. She told me everything is okay and not to worry.

There was a pedestrian hit by a car that did not stop to see his victim. The driver was in a rush and cared not if he had hit anyone, but just wanted to be on his way. The passerby pedestrians had all stopped and made a human chain in the middle of a four-way road. These humans, with their bodies, formed a shield to block the victim from being hit by another car.

People from all different ethnic backgrounds, rich and poor, had shed tears for an unknown person. A hotel employee from a nearby hotel had brought fresh blankets and pillows to help the stranger. The police came and had called his family members. One of the strangers had accompanied this unknown stranger in the ambulance and wanted to be with him as he went to the hospital.

The person that was hit was conscious and heard the crowd of people cheering and praying for him. Prayers were being held right there for him from all different faiths, for at that spot, all the people were one family. I had met my family member, as this was just a few blocks away from my apartment complex. As soon as nightfall approached, all the sights of this horrific accident were no more.

I walked my dog on that road every day, and only remembered the united front of all the unknown humans.

This one incident from my personal life had awakened me to the realization that humans have not lost humanity. I knew within us the humans, humanity hides buried within our inner souls. When a catastrophe but strikes any one of us, from the darkness all around us like dawn approaching, we see humanity but awakens.

CHAPTER SEVEN

HUMANS IN CRISIS

"Animals are known to eat their young, yet humans are extinguishing each other through hate crimes. Is this the End of Time all but predicted? Within us the humans, is but the mercy of forgiveness and within us the humans, hides but the furies of the beast. Knocking around to find safety, are but the humans in crisis."

-Ann Marie Ruby

Prayers are but sacred blessings for which we the humans unite. With the power of prayers, we find amongst us humans who guide others out of a crisis through the sacred doors of the beyond. The seers, the philosophers, the religious scholars, and the scientific scholars, all unitedly travel to find the sacred leaders for all.

On their feet they travel, and through their travel logs, they guide throughout history. The travelers united to save the citizens and the one home of the citizens, the Earth, are but the sacred world leaders. Traveling from the beginning of time, world leaders are teachers, the miracle we the citizens but seek. They are the shoulders that carry the burden as they guide all to safety, always leading the way through humanity.

The apocalypse or the End of Time has been predicted by various religious scholars. The scientific scholars also have not stayed behind as they too believe the world will come to an end with natural scientific causes. When and how this will be, is a question we the humans cannot agree upon.

There are some who do not believe in this theory at all. We all must say each individual who but enters this Earth must also leave at his or her time of departure. Today, scientists are even more worried as climate change has taken a course of its own. Some have predicted if this course continues, then the future does not look too bright.

Prophetic predictions and scientific theories lead us to contradictions, yet all come to an agreement that something is going on. We the humans must take care of our home and the planet we all but love. My concern is what about us the humans? Is it not known, take care of yourself first, then all is alright? What happens if you are no more, and your home or family but are no more? Is it then, others but enter and they continue to live a life until it is their time to depart too? So, life continues with or without us the humans, but we continue to live through all the humans we are but related to or not.

I believe we are like the animals who can be defensive and protective toward their young, but also aggressive and beastly. The difference between the humans and animals is we have intelligence to guide us. Today, however, it seems like more and more, the animal behavior is but taking over us the humans.

When a human but acts like an animal, it is by choice. The human chooses that path. It is then, they but become the beast. The human animal is but even more dangerous than the animal, for it carries the one thing that makes him or her higher than the animal, which is known as intelligence.

While doing research on the human population, I came across the most dangerous animals worldwide and saw humans had topped various lists. Animals have the capacity to kill each other, or one by one. This is how a lot of animals have become extinct. We the humans have also contributed to this extinction as now the world scientists are worried about insect extinction on top of animal extinction. Another thought that had risen within my mind is, why are humans more dangerous than animals? The reason is simple. Like I said, animals can take one by one, but we the human animals have the capacity with one gun to wipe out a herd of animals, and with one button, the complete human existence.

So, when the hunter is but hunting down the most dangerous animals within the jungles, we need to also remember you the human hunter have created this world crisis, I but call *The World Hate Crisis*. When we the humans choose to use our intelligence to create and become higher than all for the good of the society, we are all but the saving grace of this world. This is the difference between the human and the beast.

I believe we have landed upon a time when humans but choose to be the beast for selfish needs. They only see themselves in the mirror of life. They do not sit on the riverbank watching out for the lost and stranded humans who but need a helping hand. They are the destructors of this world. My prediction is they are but the awakening calls of the beast which we but have been warned about from past times.

The scientists have studied positive and negative thinking processes and their effects on the human mind. Scientists have studied the effects of the wrongful ways of life. They have predicted smoking to cause cancer, yet people still smoke. They have predicted unprotected sex to cause deadly diseases, yet people still do not pay attention. They have predicted less consumption of meat to benefit the environment and climate control, yet people still do not pay heed. They have predicted alcohol to be dangerous if taken without control, yet so many people have lost their lives to drunk drivers.

I have a horrible memory of my friend's husband being hit by a drunk driver. A few friends and I had gone to a concert as we had planned to attend this concert for days. My friend had dropped me home. Her husband, who always smiled, accompanied and had said he would take the day off tomorrow to take care of his wife as she was still recovering from a surgery. The following morning, I received a call from another friend giving me the sad news that my friend just had an apocalypse hit her life, as her husband had been hit by a drunk driver and died on spot.

I wondered why he had not just stayed home like he had planned to. The question remained a question I never asked. For my friend on that terrible morning, everything had ended because someone had chosen to drive while being intoxicated. I do not know if the driver even got any punishment or not, but a life had ended that day.

I also believe the life that had left us is in peace and it was the end of his journey. Yet for my friend, it was the beginning of a life where she had lost the reason to live within her inner soul. Yes, dawn approached, and new beginnings were ahead, yet her life would never be the same. Laws of the land forbid us to drink and drive, yet why do you choose to break the laws of the land?

Religions have also had these predictions. Do not drink without control. Do not eat more than what you can consume. Be positive and meditate. Exercise and control. Yet, we do not follow the advice from religions either.

Today, I link climate control, human behaviors, and our unaccepting of the truth to be the sole reason for our Earth's dire condition. I also link the human hate crimes to be the direct links to the apocalypse or the apocalyptic times we but have landed upon. How did I come to this conclusion, you may ask? Is it not but clear that the dinosaurs were extinct because they finished each other? Then scientifically, are we not but finishing each other?

We the humans cannot be the same, as five fingers are but different. Is it not if you are different, then you may be the victim of a hate crime? The perpetrators of the crime are the beasts that have but awakened. They were in a closed coffin, hiding their inner most feelings of hatred. They have awakened to the calls of their masters. Is it not their masters, the voice of the callers, that but walk in pride? Alone, they had no one to walk with. All are beautiful and look alike, so why should different race, color, and religion but exist?

How beautiful would the skies look without the sun, or the moon, or the stars, or the colorful rainbows? How would you but appreciate all the wonders of this Earth that but belong to The One Creator? The flowers, the green grass, or the blue ocean, all would be no more, but only you and your brothers and sisters who but look just like you would remain.

How would you but live without any other existence for when the ocean and the Earth are but no more, or the other creation of The One Creator are no more here to balance life, how would you survive? The answer is simple. You the perpetrators of the hate crimes are but solely responsible for the extinction of the human population. You like the dinosaurs, for your own nature, shall be responsible for your path and your entry to this stage of the apocalypse.

My proof is simple. According to the FBI statistics and all other data available, hate crimes have increased at a rapid rate. Worldwide, according to various reports, hate crimes are on the rise. The reports only talk about the reported crimes. People are not reporting all hate crimes and are silently taking on the bashing in fear of the mighty and the powerful hands of the wrong.

Why is it the world leaders are not paying attention to this crisis if so much data is but available to them? Is it because we cannot stop this apocalypse that but had been predicted from times ago? The philosophers, the prophets, the religious gurus, and the scientific scholars combined could not have predicted the beast but is hidden within the human souls. The prophesies have but said we would elect leaders filled with hatred to rule this Earth and that we would walk blindly behind them until someone but awakens from within to save us from our own destruction. Someone please awaken from within, to save the future even if we cannot save ourselves, to save this one world for the future generations that are not my or your blood, yet they are but our human race.

In the year 2018, we saw an increase in hate crimes for the third consecutive year within the United States. All major newspapers have come out with the same news and have predicted this is a dangerous period we but have landed upon. People are too fearful, or you might say some even feel scared or ashamed to report that they too are but victims of this crime.

Alarming reports all but have evidence, yet no one sees this is a deadly disease crippling the humans. This disease is but invisible and it is brewing within the soul of the carrier. The carriers of this disease but see not their own symptoms for they had been brewing this for years and now they have just received an open invitation to attack publicly. They are but protected within the hidden powers of the might.

I ask within the houses of the mighty powers, please awaken from within and do what is right. If Moses had walked out of the house of the Pharaoh, then you too can walk out of the homes of the perpetrators of these crimes. Awaken yourself and feel the pain and sorrows of the families of these victims who are completely innocent as they were targeted for being different. How is this but fair? Why do you but not feel for these victims? How could you the human but behave like an animal?

Is it then for you, the prophecies were but made? Are you the evil or the leader of an invisible group who but awakens from within your soul for your love of yourself? If you do love yourself, then I believe you do have some hope. Spread the same love and affection to all of the human race.

I ask the world leaders to place a blindfold on, as you but get elected. May you the elected be there for all of the inhabitants of your land that but have elected you. Do not be blind to the pain and suffering of the victims, but be blind to the differences between race, color, and religion. Do not discriminate but hold the discriminators responsible.

I ask all the world leaders to walk with a candle in your hands and glow for all. May these candles of hope spread throughout your nation, then country to country, then worldwide. May there be one huge vehicle that but can take on this calamity. May you not be deterred by the storms of this world but be there like an anchor with an ark to guide all on board to safety. Within your blessed hands, may you have the blessings to start something to eradicate *The World Hate Crisis*.

I ask you the world leaders to be like The Merciful and take over the beast as we the humans but wait for all the world leaders to unite for humanity. Guide all through your footsteps as you walk first through the fog and create a miracle for all to be guided by. Let the prophecies be there as a guide and may we the humans be able to walk in union to overcome again a crisis that is invisible, yet brewing within the most powerful creation ever created, the humans.

Be our teachers as you today awaken with humanity. Take upon your shoulders the miracles of humanity to eradicate *The World Hate Crisis*, for all around asking, seeking, and knocking are but the humans in crisis.

CHAPTER EIGHT

THE LAND AND HER LEADER

"Within all lands are but left behind the marks of the inhabitants. The land but keeps buried her historical figures, the admired, and the despised, for all throughout time. Within the pages of history are kept safely, the land and her leader."

-Ann Marie Ruby

A land houses her inhabitants. A country houses her citizens. The citizens house their leaders who are also called from the beyond and known to the beyond even before you the citizen but know of your land and your leader. The sacred travelers are but known to the seers as you have but chosen your path.

The traveler you had become as you left behind your footsteps guiding all to safety through the miracles of your journey. The teacher, you had become. The politician, you are chosen as. The miracles are hidden within your guidance as you are the wisdom guiding all out of the obstacles of this world. History takes us back through time as she teaches us the lessons of the past. Through these lessons, we are advised to either enter, or avoid the circle that had but made our ancestors commit mistakes.

Could we the humans then learn to omit the mistakes from happening all over again? Could we learn from history? Could we be guided to avoid the tunnels of obstacles, similar to the ones that had dawned upon our forefathers?

Historians walk through the pages of history to figure out these puzzles for us. They learn from the past to teach us how to walk in the future. Archeologists also dig through the past to guide us through the future as to what had gone wrong and how to avoid these calamities.

I know throughout time, the historians will write history as the archeologists uncover evidence from the past to again guide the future. How do we the humans but avoid disasters? How do we avoid becoming historical figures who people but detest, or whom archeologists find proof of as destructors of humankind?

We start at the past and let our present be guided by our own mistakes, so we do not repeat the same errors. History says Adolf Hitler was predicted by the past prophetic figures, yet we the inhabitants of the land still elected him to be our guide and leader. He had said,

"I don't see much future for the Americans. In my view, it's a decayed country. And they have their racial problem, and the problem of social inequalities [...] But my feelings against Americanism are feelings of hatred and deep repugnance. I feel myself more akin to any European country, no matter which. Everything about the behavior of American society reveals that it's half Judaised, and the other half negrified. How can one expect a State like that to hold together […]?" (145).

Why are we allowing the words of a dictator to come face us in the truth of daylight as we awaken within the worst statistics? Why are we allowing his words to but stare at our face? I do not agree with the words of a dictator, and I shall walk for you, with you.

I shall love, honor, and hold on to the different faces throughout eternity as my rainbow of blessed children of the world. I have awakened myself first. Now, I call to awaken you. For how long will you reject my call of love?

We had also chosen Mahatma Gandhi to lead in another land. I do so wish we had more wise men like him as Gandhi had famously said, "I suppose leadership at one time meant muscles; but today it means getting along with people" ("Mahatma Gandhi").

Just read the different quotations by the two leaders you the humans had but elected. One was trying to unite all, and the other was trying to divide all. Does this mean all of their decisions were right or wrong?

I was not there, so I cannot say. History reminds us one was a humanitarian, and the other was an inhumane dictator who only divided us the humans. Inflicted words of the world leaders can harm and create division amongst the humans as history through the time machine is but a witness through the tales told.

Words said cannot be taken back as they remain frozen throughout time for all to witness. If these words can harm or divide amongst even one group, then I wonder why a land would pick this leader to rule her. From time to time, we are blessed with sacred leaders or humanitarians who are born to unite this world in times of crises.

Some call them spiritual gurus. Some call them gifts to humankind. I but call them humans with humanity. What about the opposite of a humanitarian? The inhumane who is but selfish and egoistic, who sees nothing but his or her own reflection within the mirror of life?

They only know if it but hurts themselves or not. They feel not of your pain or your joys of life. They are but the creators of division worldwide and wash away shore after shore, only keeping an eye over their own personal belongings.

Remember when you but follow them, it is only hours before your home too shall be struck by their floods of anger. Your homes shall wash away like all on this inhumane person's path. His or her taught lessons shall but break down all of your children and the future generations too.

Remember these destructive behaviors are all built upon the sand. These houses that you so proudly build are but sandcastles which shall have head stones placed upon them as you and your self-created destructive storm but pass away. These headstones but shall say:

Buried beneath is but the lost humanity of humans who had awakened to hate.

The only remaining building that shall last throughout eternity is but the humanitarian buildings that had protected all throughout the storms of life. These buildings are the praying hands of a human who but sheltered all throughout the storms under his or her humanitarian umbrella.

Yes, there shall be headstones placed here too, but a tree shall grow from here representing the parental figure of the humanitarians. Under this tree shall appear again, new beginnings and new endings. Stories shall be written and rewritten throughout time.

Today, we have all ended upon a time where division but creates another brewing storm. Innocent lives are being washed away for being different. Race, color, and religion are but under attack. The waves of the ocean are reaching shore as she is washing away all that but is in her way. I watch people jumping into this sinful ocean with absolutely no fear.

It has become a game of dare. Whoever wants to join can join. Like thunder, the mighty mouth of evil and the forceful are but their voices. Like lightning bolts, they are appearing and falling all over. Like wildfires, they have but spread. I ask myself, what can we do? Is there no hope left for us the humans with humanity?

We should avoid all the crimes and control them. Hate crimes should not even exist for this is a crime that should be reported and not accepted by the human race. This crime is an invisible virus that but leads to all crimes combined. A hate crime is the king or queen of all crimes.

One day, I was walking my dog in Orlando, Florida. I saw a young child about seven years old was being ridiculed within my neighborhood. It was a very private resort type neighborhood where we had various ethnic groups residing.

I watched a group of girls pull the shorts of a girl who I thought was playing with them. They were making fun of her as they asked why she had leggings under her shorts, and why she always covered up. They told her Muslims are bad and asked why she was a Muslim.

I ran and held on to the child as I thought, not in my land. You will not instigate any hatred within my land. I wondered how these young children were even capable of realizing differences.

What were they being taught at home or even at school? I asked myself, what can I do? How can I alone unite all race, color, and religion into one group, the humans with humanity?

Any or all global leaders chosen by the land should not instigate this kind of crimes. Within this path, history shall again be made. All the prophecies of apocalyptic times shall but come to land. This shall be the End of Time for peace and justice for all.

Throughout history, we the humans have divided within our opinions even amongst the worst crises. With the climate crisis, we still have divisions, yet some powerful hands are trying to fight climate change. We must now unite and fight against the next apocalypse, *The World Hate Crisis*.

I ask all of you the world leaders to awaken yourself for peace and harmony. From within each one of you, oh the leaders of this world, can I just have a small amount of love, honor, and justice for the victims of all the hate crimes of this world?

Dwight D. Eisenhower, the 34th President of the United States, said in his Second Inaugural Address, "We seek peace, knowing that peace is the climate of freedom."

Mother Teresa had said, "Today, if we have no peace, it is because we have forgotten that we belong to each other—that man, that woman, that child is my brother, my sister" (330).

I again ask who but can lead us out of this situation? Personally, I have not been affected, yet my inner soul feels like I have been affected through the teardrops of all the hate crime victims. I see the salty water that but falls from all the victims has become the bathing place for you the perpetrators.

I know there is a person who shall walk with me on my quest to find this freedom for all the victims that have been affected and all of you who but shall be affected if we do not unite and find a solution. Again, the land but chooses her leader as you the inhabitant but wish for him or her. I know the thought is scary as I can hear the wise saying, "Beware what you wish for."

This sacred soul again but asks all to unite under one tree, the tree of humanity. I believe there is only One Creator. We are but the creation also known as the human race, who but come from the one tree of The Creator of all.

I ask you the perpetrators of this crime. I ask you all the powerful attackers, is it not your Creator who but created this human you but attack? Therefore, who are you attacking? Your victim or your Creator?

Today, you the human awaken to my call as we choose one leader who can unite all world leaders to walk for the humans who are facing a crisis, known as *The World Hate Crisis*. Through the blessed guidance of the world leaders, we shall find the door of miracles. Let the teachers and the politicians in union hold on to all of the citizens of this one Earth and lead all to safety.

The Earth is but our mother we all unite for, as she is but our final resting place. We the humans select or reject our world leaders as they but prove themselves. History and the historical figures through their footsteps create a path for all to follow as we learn from the past, to live within the present, and guide the future accordingly. World leaders are the anchors who in union guide all throughout time. When all become no more, and nothing is but left, even then from the pages of history are still very much alive, the land and her leader.

CHAPTER NINE

CONSTRUCTIVE CRITICISM

"On the stage you but stand taking on the sharp tongues of the critics, for your love for them outweighs the pain from their hurtful words, their constructive criticism."

-Ann Marie Ruby

The human mind but criticizes all that is not known or for the lack of knowledge given or received. When miracles from the beyond but take form, we know even the sharp tongues have no constructive criticism for all but agree, miracles are just that, miracles. When these miracles, however, are given in the form of words, they are just words left within the air.

The protective shield of the invisible force created through words of wisdom is but all my love for this world. I search for the path and the footsteps laid behind by the politicians as an invisible miracle from the land for her children. Throughout time, these leaders place themselves as a shield to only protect all from getting hurt from the known and unknown calamities beyond human control. The sacred leaders are left within the pages of wisdom as history teaches all the future generations from the footsteps of these leaders.

All throughout my life, I had chosen to stay within the audience as that is where I feel comfortable. To be loved and to be appreciated are the biggest gifts this world can but give a person. I always say, "Please do not say anything if your voice but leaves dried teardrops upon the pillowcases overnight." This is my personality as I but walk away from any confrontation or any unjust words spilled upon my soul.

When and wherever I had been attacked with the voices or unjust actions of an attacker, I had chosen to walk away in fear. I have awakened to this stage of my life where now I can say, "No." I will stand up and say, "No more shall you but hurt me." I have gotten out of my cave and have told the wrongdoers I shall but fight for my right and will not accept any wrongdoing within my home or around me.

I feel to be on the stage and take constructive criticism for the love of the humans and humanity, one must be strong not to fall from the attacks of the unknown critics. To lead a war, one must not only be a strong warrior but a teacher who can guide you to walk away without any harsh feelings. My sacred eyes and soul but seek a strong human with humanity, who is an anchor, and shall not move or tilt even when the inhumane humans but shout.

I am the candle that shall burn for you. With the first gust of wind, I need support to lean upon or a foundation to stand on. I need strong hands who but shall be my candle holder. The candle holder shall be like the ark I can stand on, from where I can ask the humans to awaken. It shall be a strong shoulder I can lean upon even when you strike me for talking about the truth and standing up for the truth.

114

I search for the strong set of hands that shall be my walking stick, giving me support as I become frail by the knocks of the unjust words of the wrong. I ask for a world leader, a person who is but a human with humanity. Stand with me and be my support, for I know, you too but cry for peace and justice. You can be the powerful voice of humanity. You will not fall or collapse as the inhumane voices but come as a storm to harm you. I shall be there holding on to you and all the sacred world leaders as we the citizens back you up for the rights of a citizen.

I realize as my dreams have guided me to my pen and paper, I am but the author who must ask, seek, and knock through my books. I must be there through my prayers. May my wisdom be there to guide you and awaken you to humanity.

My hope is to find the Earthly soul of the one who will awaken for the sake of humanity. I seek your help and wisdom as you can be on that stage fighting to get back the honor, dignity, and courage of all the victims of *The World Hate Crisis*. I have asked my soul over and over again, where do I but find this person? Who do I ask to help me within this unseen, yet deadly disease that but grows wildly as an unknown virus? I know within my dreams, I have some clues as to where I should begin this part of my journey.

The Netherlands is a small European country where my dreams but have guided me to. I had stood in front of the Peace Palace and saw how the International Court of Justice is sitting there to bring peace and justice to all of whom are but wronged. I asked myself, what about the victims of the hate crimes? What about this deadly disease that is brewing all around this world?

When I was in the Netherlands, I was again bothered by the worldwide hate crimes becoming an epidemic, if not controlled. I know the world has started to organize and report these hate crimes. These days, crimes are being reported, but unreported cases still outweigh the reported ones.

Reported crimes make the statistics, yet the unreported crimes are stored within the memories of the beholders. I often wonder what the unreported crimes are and why people are afraid to report these crimes. I had witnessed a small incident that had bothered me for a long time. I was staying in an extended stay hotel when I had moved to Seattle. After breakfast, I was walking in the hallway.

An elderly couple had moved into the suite next door to me. I watched the woman walk past me and talk to a young child who was around ten years old. She asked the child if the child could come and clean their room as it needed some more vacuuming. The young child started to cry because of what the woman was saying. The mother of the child ran outside and had an argument with the woman. The elderly couple was Caucasian, and the young family was Indian.

The first thing the elderly woman had said was she just assumed they were cleaners and asked what she did wrong. I watched the child break into a sob. Why did the woman think she was a cleaning woman when she was just a child?

I saw the Indian mother take hold of her child and go inside the room. The elderly woman who smiled at me and winked her eye had walked back to her husband. He had asked her why she had done that. She said she thought the family looked Hispanic.

I had to get involved. I have seen racist people, but even after having traveled all around the globe, I have never seen a racist put down a young child. This woman was unjustly putting some people down for her fun. I asked her, "Why?"

I watched her husband look at her in shock. I told her, "So, you are a racist and you wanted to crush a child and her hopes." I asked her, "What is wrong with being a maid, waiter, or the people you the rich need to survive with your luxurious lifestyles?"

She then left without another word. I did not know who she was, or anything about her except that I had seen hatred in the worst kind as this hatred was directed toward an innocent child. I could never understand why this was so, but I wonder if she understood.

I knew the mother of the child did not want any argument arising from this situation as I saw her innocently walk away. I knew this was a very sad day when a person has this kind of feeling. My inner question is, why are people afraid to say anything and stand up peacefully?

My thoughts will always bother me. Will this child grow up in fear? Or will she have anger buried within her? As a stranger, I did not want to get involved either. But, then am I being unjust, or do I just want to save myself and walk away? I guess these small frictions need to be resolved for us to wake up as a society. We need to be able to speak up. So, I have taken pen to paper as my fight against hate crimes.

Dawn breaks open each morning with or without personal suffering. This world now has people who have awakened to their inner hatred that has grown out of their homes and are but attacking each other. Innocent people are being attacked for being at the wrong place at the wrong time.

My eyes search for a human who will want to stand up for these innocent souls. I stood near the statue of William the Silent in The Hague, and wondered how the world leaders stand on the stage and deal with all the crises they but have upon them. I know to face all of the critics in front of you and still smile for the sake of a nation is but the most honorable job on Earth. Today, I only have the words and wisdom of the past leaders, who had united their nation for the sake of their own land and her citizens.

I wonder where I shall find a person who will want to unite all the humans of this world for the sake of humanity. I cry for all the victims spread around the globe who are attacked for being of a different race, color, religion, sexual orientation, gender, or for just being different. These inhumane hate crimes should be considered the biggest crimes on this Earth.

How do you the judged but judge someone for being different? How do we awaken the racist to his or her own mischiefs and wrongdoings? What if we record your own crimes and show your family and your future generations? Would you then awaken? Or has this been brewing within your inner soul too long for you to awaken from?

From the past wisdom of the wise and the messages left by the world leaders, the philosophers, and the religious gurus, we all know the End of Time but comes upon us. The human hate crimes, and the division or the different opinions of the humans that these situations but expose may just be our way to the Earth's ending stage. World Wars have taken away so much from our Earth. Even to this day, we have so much division amongst us.

Today, we have upon us a crisis that is but driving us apart. We need to be guided by our past and take our present to the future, safely. I have placed pen to paper to bring to light the criminals, the instigators, and the perpetrators who hide within us the humans. They can be even within you the reader. So, I ask the world to unite and help eradicate this hatred that leads to hate crimes. I ask the world leaders to unite within the land where the Peace Palace but stands to lead us the united world citizens through this stage of our lives.

I shall always be there supporting all throughout the days and throughout the nights. I need a strong hand of support who will be there to hold on to my candles lighted through the worst windstorms. I believe in the words of the 40th President of the United States, Ronald Reagan, "Peace is not absence of conflict, it is the ability to handle conflict by peaceful means." I know at this stage, we need people who can talk to their enemies without worrying about being criticized, without moving from their grounds, the grounds of the right.

We need the world to guide and unite for the sake of the human souls. All humans must open their eyes and see how this crisis but is the apocalypse. If not controlled, then this is but the apocalyptic stage we are moving into.

During another time period when the world but faced World War II, Winston Churchill said, "If the human race wishes to have a prolonged and indefinite period of material prosperity, they have only got to behave in a peaceful and helpful way toward one another" ("Winston Churchill").

Today, we seek for yet another world leader who would take this apocalypse as a fight and be victorious. The stage is there with the philosophical, historical, political, and scientific warriors who but unite through the wisdom and the wise.

I know I shall be victorious as I believe there are world leaders who too stay awake only to keep all within the safety of their guidance. They walk ahead to make sure all is but clear. They guide all through the blessed miracles of their wisdom. The path is blessed as the travelers are following the sacred traveler, the leader, the teacher, and the blessed shield who but takes on all obstacles for the love of the land.

In union, this world shall but guide us to the hands of the person or people who shall guide us out of *The World Hate Crisis*. These leaders are but great as they take upon their shoulders, the love and the constructive criticism.

CHAPTER TEN

UMBRELLA OF PROTECTION

"From the heavy apocalyptic storms, guide us out the sacred world leaders who but stand united. It is their hands that but become our umbrella of protection."

-Ann Marie Ruby

How do we but protect what is not known to us? How do we see what has not yet become? We ask, seek, and knock upon the umbrella of protection of the Heavens above for miracles. Always, we have amongst us, the seers who are there to guide us throughout time. These sacred souls but in union with all the known and unknown travelers unite within the bond of humanity to form an umbrella of protection for all humans alike.

Walking ahead to guide all through the obstacles and the darkness of the night are but the sacred world leaders, the sacred teachers, and the sacred scholars of all time. Like the guiding lighthouse, they walk ahead, always keeping the lanterns burning for all whom but follow behind. The sacred politicians are but true teachers as they always keep an eye out for all the travelers following behind.

The sacred caretakers they become, and their travel journey is the lantern glowing throughout time to guide all even from the pages of history. We have, however, always found within ourselves the negative characters throughout history, from which we the humans but need protection. We at this stage need to find the umbrella of protection.

Walking through the statistics of the hate crisis, I see this crisis has been brewing slowly, yet as more time flies by, the crisis is becoming a catastrophe. I have watched the wild storms brewing in the Caribbean Sea. They take birth as a small storm and convert to a natural disaster.

No life is spared as the hurricanes are but blind. They take along all that but come upon their path. No mercy is but given here as we only take shelter within the shelters provided by our respective governments.

Like the astrological scholars of yesteryears who could predict without advance science, today meteorologists can predict and guide us through storms. Likewise, the scientists can predict some of the climate changes and their effects to avoid the catastrophes upon the human race. Here within the invisible force of *The World Hate Crisis*, we have nothing but the worldwide statistics.

These statistics show us we are heading toward a catastrophic and apocalyptic storm that is brewing within the inner souls of the humans without humanity. Aside from the statistics and all the reported records, we were also guided by the prophets, as well as scientific scholars. The prophecies were that the End of Time but shall arrive upon our doors.

The scientific scholars have agreed that the world's climate changes might become catastrophic if not controlled.

126

The climate changes shall lead to End of Time. Science also agrees if the inner feelings of a person are not controlled, the situation could become dangerous.

What but happens if the situation is not taken under control? What if the situation is being inflicted by the powerful people and groups who but grow within hatred? What happens when we the humans face this apocalypse within our lifetime? What does a person do when all around the Earth, darkness but fills from personal hatred that but overshadows the skies and converts this world into a dark stormy night? The world's hate crime report looks very bleak.

A person today walking out of his or her home fears what if tonight he or she is but attacked? The parents lighting candles to pray, keep the candles burning until their children but return home. Not for being at the wrong place, and not for doing anything wrong, but for being different than your attacker is but your fault.

The attackers praying within their respective worshipping places should think how is it you but pray to your Creator on this night? Do you but ask why The Creator had created different humans? Why do we have different sized fingers on our hands? What is it that bothers you that you have learned to hate the different?

I had another experience that would bother me for a long time. I had walked into a spa to get my hair and nails done as I really enjoy my time in the spa. I had chosen a different spa than my regular one as I could not find any openings within my schedule.

I had walked in with a nice Hindu family who also had their appointments before mine. As we walked in, I was offered the first available seat, even though I had reminded them the other family was before me. As I entered the nail salon section, I watched the Hindu family in an argument with the hairdresser.

I watched how the hairdresser had belittled the Indian family and told them she cannot believe Hinduism is even allowed to be practiced in this country. The Indian family had reminded her they were U.S. citizens and were third generation Americans, yet the hairdresser who was the owner of the spa was not even a U.S. citizen.

I wondered, now these disagreements and racial divisions are but in the open air. I asked why this was happening. I know these feelings were buried within the human souls and now were being brought out.

I do not believe you wake up one day and you just become a racist. There is a storm brewing all around us and we must do something before this storm but becomes an apocalyptic war. I did my share in this situation as I never went back to this spa.

I had seen the reviews and realized a lot of people had felt the owners were racist and left their remarks as to this effect. I was very upset at the spa owners, yet I felt amazingly good realizing like myself, a lot of customers saw this truth. I realized aside from racist people, there are also goodhearted people all around this globe.

I guess my unanswered questions were given some hope through the great words of yet another world leader, as Nelson Mandela had said,

"No one is born hating another person because of the color of his skin or his background or his religion. People must learn to hate, and if they can learn to hate, they can be taught to love, for love comes more naturally to the human heart than its opposite" (622).

What an honorable person he was with such a positive thought and hope for all of us whom but cry for the united human race. I would say even if you cannot accept the difference, then still do not hate the others for being different. Let the paths be different as we the humans but walk in peace.

The destination may be different, yet the journey is the same as we all but have one entry and one exit. All that shall remain is but the headstone on the sands of the traveled paths. I ask all of the world leaders today to unite on a journey to eradicate *The World Hate Crisis.*

I have seen the world leaders walk in union to eradicate the obstacles of this world. I have seen the world leaders sit with strangers and hold their hands as they too had tears fall for the unknown strangers. I have seen the world leaders staying awake to make sure their citizens are but safe within their respective lands. I also have seen the same world leaders send their best wishes when a disaster but hits a foreign land of another world leader.

Why is it these world leaders stay awake and try to help each other throughout all the hurdles the other but faces? Today, the sacred world leaders please unite once again for this world and the dire crisis she is but facing as all the children of Mother Earth are facing a silent killer that is but invisible. In union, I know you the world leaders will be able to take control of this storm.

Hold on to the ark in union and there shall be peace and harmony as you but bring this sacred ark back to safety. Let the humans have a mirror of reflection left for all the criminals of this world as they too see their own reflections and realize what have they but done. This world also must hold these crimes to be held as the biggest crimes committed by the humankind.

I will ask all of you the world leaders to begin this blessed journey as you unite. Let one person lead this journey as all of you unite under this umbrella of the united leaders of the world. I search for the world leader who but shall volunteer to take up this crisis for the humans of this one world. Within our world, there is only one race and one religion and one ethnicity. I call this the humans with humanity.

Today, I, the unknown and the unheard voice of a human, but call upon all the sacred world leaders to unite under this crisis and maybe we can unite under one house of peace to eradicate *The World Hate Crisis*. This world but gives birth to world leaders with humanity.

Some leaders become historical. Some names, however, get wiped away throughout time. I believe amongst all of you, I shall find the one my heart but searches for who shall for the sake of humanity unite all humans with their own humanity.

Under the protection of our great teachers, the world leaders, we shall find our path to safety. Always follow the footsteps of the great leaders as they create a blessed path for you. Yet, keep your eyes open and make sure you do not follow blindly as then it is you who but shall fall. The leaders are the sacred travelers who walk for all whom need their protection.

You too are but a traveler who needs to walk on your own feet, guided by the sacred leaders for whom you have a safe path to travel upon. Safe you shall be, if only you too keep an eye out for the sacred leaders, not the lost and stranded leaders. How can a lost traveler but guide? Ask yourself, before you decide to follow.

We the humans are but the greatest creation in this world. Let us in union stand up and show the future we are but the greatest creation. When all of this world does come to an end, even then, may we the humans be able to stand tall and strong and say we are, were, and shall always be the greatest creation of The One Creator.

It is The Lord who but guides us as we decide to follow our chosen world leaders. May we have sacred blessed souls, and always know the weight of our decision is upon each individual soul. I know we shall in union for the right reason, under the right world leader's guidance, eradicate *The World Hate Crisis*.

Recently, I watched within the Netherlands, students had skipped school to walk for climate control. They said they have begun by separating their own trash and recycling. I saw a lot of these children had also become vegan or vegetarians because eating less meat would help climate control.

I watched with so much love and honor for these children as they walked in union. I realized we do have hope within the hands of these children. They love this Mother Earth and are fighting for her. How could they not love each other, the children of this one world?

I know the inner sacred love of us the citizens for all of the citizens of this world is also brewing within our sacred souls. We just need to brew this love faster than any hate crimes. In union, we the children of this world shall be victorious as we keep the lanterns of hope burning for all of the citizens of the past, the present, and the future to be guided by. With hand in hand we shall again bless all the citizens of this world as we place our footprints upon the same path united with the world leaders, to eradicate *The World Hate Crisis* as the world leaders become our umbrella of protection.

FINAL CHAPTER

CHART OF *THE WORLD HATE CRISIS*

"Not just the words of a soul, but the fingerprint left behind by the criminal talks for itself. It is stamped permanently within the paths traveled by the victims who cannot talk for themselves, yet talking on their behalf is but the chart of The World Hate Crisis"

-Ann Marie Ruby

On February 20, 2019, as I landed upon this chapter, a U.S. coast guard officer in Maryland, responsible to protect our land and her children, has been apprehended. His crime is that he wanted to have a white nation. His inner wish was to wipe out the rest of the population. He was plotting a mass terrorist attack. He believed within his hands, he had the resources and would just need to plan. He was stopped by other people who were also in charge of protecting this nation. My fear is, what if he had been successful? Is this again another sign from the beyond guiding us to unite and eradicate *The World Hate Crisis*?

As you have walked through this book, and finally ended upon this chapter, you know here rest the charts created by us the humans for we placed ourselves upon the charts. I ask you, keep my words within your soul. I guide you not for today, but for tomorrow which has been shown to me for I see the charts of the future.

I am only able to show you the charts of yesteryears which are available to the human eyes. Believe in the miracles and know guidance is only given for protection. I am not a doctor, so I cannot prescribe any medication. I call myself a dream psychic for I am blessed to have dreams of the future, not of today.

How am I able to stop the future? Sometimes, I avoid things that are in my capacity for I know danger lies ahead. Sometimes, they just come upon me and there is absolutely nothing I can do, yet I knew the situation that was to come. Thus, the collision is far less than what it would have been. That is where this book had come from and taken birth for.

It is not what is today, but what we humans without any miracle of the beyond can avoid, so our future generation can find themselves a brighter tomorrow. The End of Time has been predicted but let our future generation have a chance and let us in union avoid all man-made catastrophes. Our gift is love. Our weapon of destruction is hatred. In union, let us end *The World Hate Crisis*.

Throughout time, the path and the travelers are there to guide us. It is our own decision who we follow and how we follow. The miracles are always there for the believers as the teachers, known to all as the world leaders, are standing on the stage to guide us. History recalls how amongst these chosen world leaders, we the citizens have chosen wrong leaders over and over to only regret as time guides us to the truth. Throughout time, as the world comes to the brink of collapse or human lives are at risk, we find amongst ourselves miracles that take birth from the beyond. We find miracles in the form of blessed guides, also known as blessed world leaders, to be reborn again.

Like a lighthouse guiding all who are lost within a tsunami, comes the lighthouse keepers. It is that time again, when we must choose yet another group of world leaders, sacred teachers, or just humans with humanity, to guide us upon the right path, away from the tsunami, onto the safe shores of humanity. As I created charts from my own research through the available statistics of human hate crimes, I have realized how fragile life is.

The victims of these crimes had no fault of their own, yet they had one thing in common, they were all different from their attackers. Why is it you the criminal think you are but greater than even The Creator? For is it not that you are but a creation? Then, why is it that you the judged but become The Judge?

At the end of this chapter, I have only included a few charts with data that was available to me for hate crime incidents. There is no perfect data, as most of the crimes go unreported. If only all the victims openly report without fearing the hunters, then we can resolve this catastrophic crisis. As you go over the charts I have put together, please awaken yourselves from within. Do not take my charts as a guide. Please do the research for yourself and find out the buried truth hidden within the dividers of our society. Find out how many have been affected by these devastating acts and how these acts have devasted families.

The long-term effects these families will have to go through because of one hate crime is unthinkable. The numbers only prove we the humans have a crisis upon our hands. The numbers can never justify why a life has to be remembered as a number and not remembered by the achievements of his or her life.

Awaken your inner self as you hold on to your newborn child within your hands today. A mother just buried her child today because he or she became a number someone did not like. How is this fair? Forgive me for even going there, for all of these crimes are against my basic moral values. I ask you the family of the victims for forgiveness, as within my soul, you are the brave traveler whose journey has awakened humans with humanity.

Today, I create this chart to awaken all humans with humanity. I only hope all sacred souls throughout this globe realize this is a crisis we can but eradicate if we only awaken within humanity. I ask the world leaders to step up in union to take another look at this crisis. This crisis will take over all other world crises as we are but brewing this crisis within our inner souls.

I have seen many world leaders throughout my travels within this world. I have spoken to many, yet I know only one world leader who had come and held me up when I was about to fall. I will forever remember that moment as I only pray, we have more world leaders like you, who are but humans with humanity.

Maybe the honorable Prime Minister Mark Rutte can be involved within this effort to eradicate the world from all divisions. With support from you, and all other world leaders, we can bring an end to this one crisis we all but face in union. Please join me and support this as we but in union end *The World Hate Crisis*.

The annual Churchill Lecture in Zurich, Switzerland was being held as I was finishing chapter nine of my book. Prime Minister Mark Rutte gave the Churchill lecture at the University of Zurich. I heard a world leader call upon all the world leaders and upon all the organizations like the European Union, United Nations, World Trade Organization, International Monetary Fund, and all others to unite. Prime Minister Mark Rutte has touched upon a huge subject that I completely support and agree with. I believe this is a sign that is being sent out by The Lord. He has talked about his viewpoint in his Churchill lecture. As a spiritual person, I always try to find positive vibes of union around the globe.

Prime Minister Mark Rutte, in his lecture, said, "we should stick together, now more than ever. Because if the chaos of Brexit teaches us anything, it's that there's no such thing as splendid isolation." I believe in miracles and I believe so does Prime Minister Mark Rutte. Other than that, I have no idea why a world leader would touch upon a topic I have been seeking for all around to find support within, that too, at the same time I am finishing up my book. I know if all the world leaders unite, this issue will be resolved.

We must talk about how we the citizens of the world should unite and in union, we shall resolve all obstacles that come upon us, like *The World Hate Crisis*. Maybe, we can all agree to have zero tolerance for the perpetrators of hate crimes. I ask all world leaders to unite and call upon a universal law which will unite all countries in a united treaty. The treaty will protect the victims and call out against all hate crimes universally, as unacceptable. This world will find peace upon the united shoulders of all ethnicities.

As I conclude my book, I ask all the blessed leaders of this world and all the humans who but select the world leaders, please today in union let us call for a peace treaty around this globe. Place your signature upon this treaty and ask all to unitedly seek justice for *The World Hate Crisis*, by making this a universal law. May the International Court of Justice, also be involved and help us the citizens of this world as we in union pass this law.

We the citizens of the past, present, and future, should not accept or forgive any perpetrators of hate crimes for this is a violation of the human birthright. May this law be accepted throughout this globe. May we again sleep in peace with open windows and doors bringing in the breeze of peace and harmony. I pray we can eradicate this crisis as we walk through the charts of *The World Hate Crisis*.

Love and victory will be upon the united front of all humans. Throughout my book, I want all to know hate crimes have always existed, yet we had kept this inner hatred within control. If you travel through the pages of history, you will see hate crimes had increased at certain periods and then went down again. By studying these time periods, we may be able to decide what we had done wrong to increase the hate crime incidents.

A doctor needs to find the source and then prescribe the medication to cure these problems. I ask the world leaders to find the source first as you study history and the time periods when hate crimes had increased. United, we the humans will be able to resolve this crisis through the united efforts of the sacred minds of the sacred leaders who but wish to resolve this crisis before it gets out of control.

I only hope the world leaders give us the support to openly face the perpetrators of these crimes, without the fear of retaliation. Hold on to the hands of the victims as the victims but cry upon your shoulders for help through my pen and paper. Let us walk through some of these crimes. It is clear, these crimes are increasing and shall only increase as the perpetrators are openly attacking as they are the might of a society. I know within your hands, oh the sacred leaders, but rests the future of this one world. May the path be there as we follow these world leaders to guide us to safety.

I ask the world leaders, and the humans who only think about today, awaken to tomorrow when all shall be dark, and dawn shall not come to welcome us. Brew within your inner soul, love for yourself. With your eyes, see all humans as yourself in different forms and colors. My prediction is all shall come to an end as all had come to

144

begin. In peace, let us begin to end *The World Hate Crisis* in union. Let this catastrophe not become World War III. World War II had begun with the invasion of lands, but ended with the invasion of human rights.

The catastrophic storm of World War II had intensified through the personal hatred of one single individual for others not like him. This complete book and the values instilled within this book is everything this historical figure was against, as he was one of the biggest instigators of world hate crimes that has ever set foot upon this Earth. Let us not awaken another Hitler now and give birth to World War III. Why was it we the humans of the past did not see the hate crimes of World War II until they became catastrophic? Humans with humanity had to be awakened in union to fight this war.

My prediction is that we the humans are on a path to extinction because of *The World Hate Crisis*. The insects are on the path to extinction as we are not able to save them but have a hand in extinguishing them. The animals have suffered extinction as from prehistoric times to current days, they but attack each other on top of we the human hunters hunting them down to become extinct.

We the humans have bred within our inner soul, hatred gathered toward others unlike us and are taking this sacred world to the stage of extinction. Are you the human worried about a wild animal attacking you? Please do not forget about the wild beastly human with an individual gun and its capacity to take multiple lives at once.

I ask the humans of the present, awaken yourself today. Let us not give birth to World War III for amongst our fingertips, we have biological, chemical, and weapons of mass destruction which would wipe out this world with the press of a button. This button would make the human population extinct in one go. Remember, even without all of these advanced technologies, World War II consumed an estimated loss of up to 85 million victims. So, please, I call upon the human individuals, the world leaders, the peace keepers, and all humans to awaken to my call for humanity.

Let us not wipe out the future of the next generations. Within my dream, I had heard a wise man kept on saying, "Work for each other, not against each other." May this catastrophe not become the sole reason of extinction of the human race. Let us in union eradicate *The World Hate Crisis*.

CHART OF *THE WORLD HATE CRISIS*

Oh sacred leaders, through your footsteps,

Guide us, oh the tour guides of this world.

Oh the politicians throughout history,

You are but miracles from the beyond as you teach

To use the same weighing scale for all.

You make sure humanity but awakens within all

Humans in crisis as we face this catastrophic war.

You, the land and her leader, protect us for you

Take on the constructive criticism as you become

The umbrella of protection for all, through the

CHART OF *THE WORLD HATE CRISIS*.

Hate Crimes by Bias in the USA
(1996-2017)

The following chart is a representation of hate crimes in the USA from 1996 to 2017 based on data from the FBI. The line shows the number of hate crime incidents each year. The bars show the total number of hate crimes, stacked by category, or bias, every year. The majority of the incidents are a result of race/ethnicity/ancestry bias.

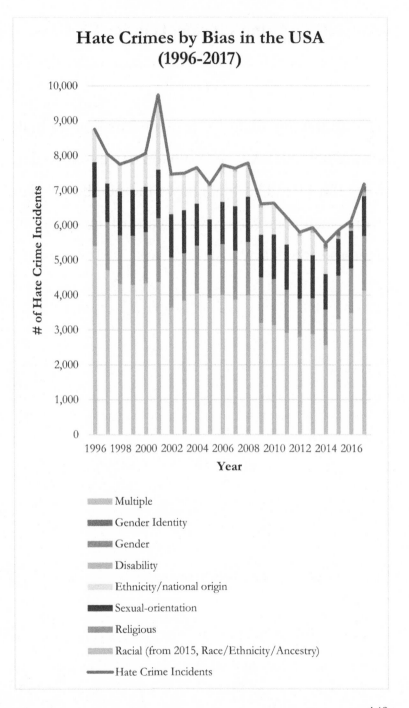

Hate Crimes Incidents in the USA
(1996-2017)

The following chart is a representation of hate crimes in the USA from 1996 to 2017 based on data from the FBI. The line shows the number of hate crime incidents each year. Years of increase and decrease are clearly visible.

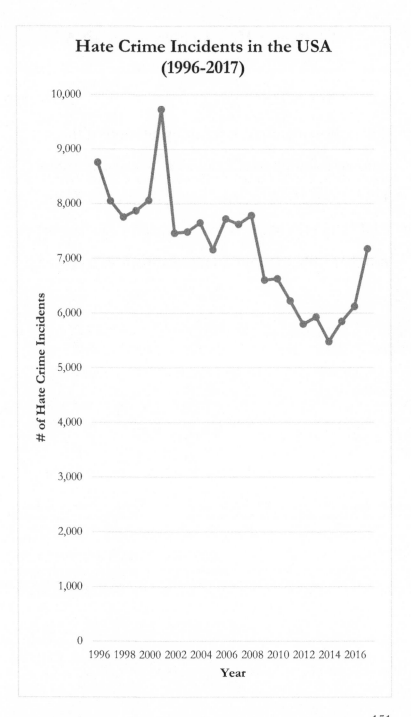

Change in Hate Crimes in the USA
(1996-2017)

The following chart is a representation of the change in number of hate crime incidents in the USA from 1996 to 2017 based on data from the FBI. The bars show the increase and decease in number of hate crime incidents from year to year.

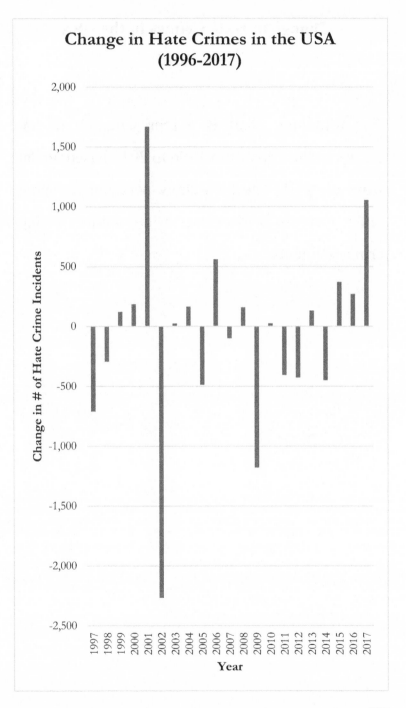

Change in Hate Crimes in the USA
(1996-2017)

The following chart is a representation of hate crimes in the USA from 1996 to 2017 based on data from the FBI. The bars show percentage change, either increase or decrease, in the number of hate crime incidents.

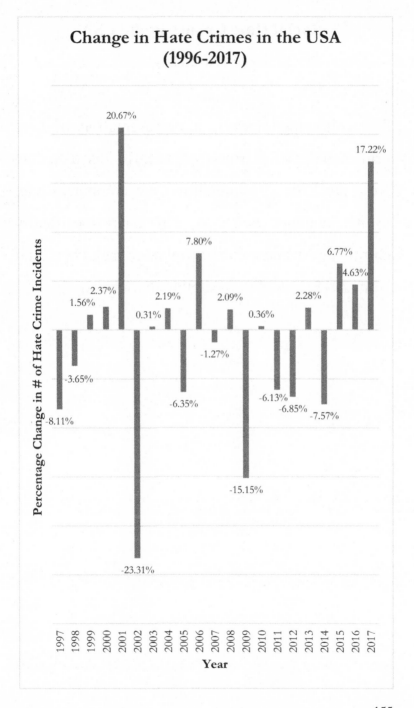

Racial Hate Crimes in the USA
(1996-2017)

The following chart is a representation of hate crimes in the USA from 1996 to 2017 based on data from the FBI. The line shows the number of hate crime incidents each year. This chart specifically shows hate crime incidents linked to racial bias, and from 2015, linked to race/ethnicity/ancestry bias.

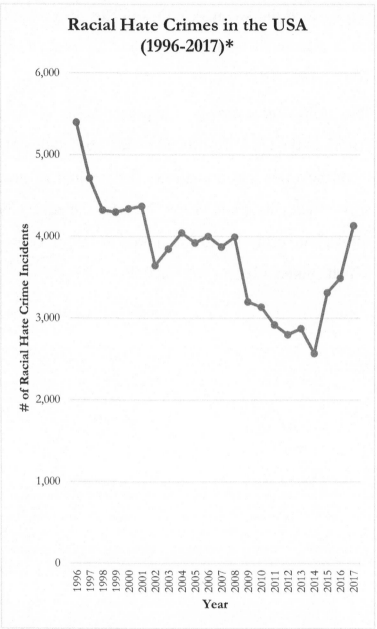

Racial Hate Crimes in the USA (1996-2017)*

*From 2015, includes Race, Ethnicity, and Ancestry biases.

Religious Hate Crimes in the USA
(1996-2017)

The following chart is a representation of hate crimes in the USA from 1996 to 2017 based on data from the FBI. The line shows the number of hate crime incidents each year. This chart specifically shows hate crime incidents linked to religious bias which spiked after the 9/11 attacks.

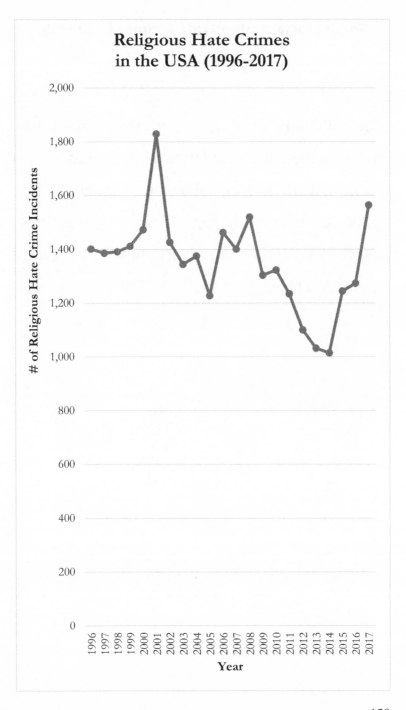

**Religious Hate Crimes
in the USA (1996-2017)**

Sexual Orientation Hate Crimes in the USA
(1996-2017)

The following chart is a representation of hate crimes in the USA from 1996 to 2017 based on data from the FBI. The line shows the number of hate crime incidents each year. This chart specifically shows hate crime incidents linked to sexual orientation bias.

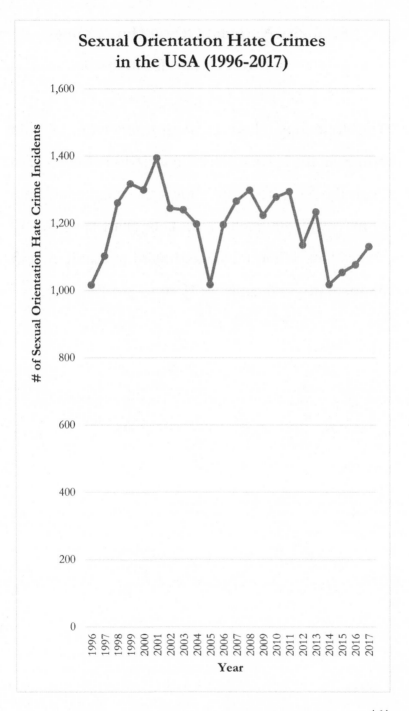

Ethnicity/National Origin Hate Crimes
in the USA (1996-2017)

The following chart is a representation of hate crimes in the USA from 1996 to 2014 based on data from the FBI. The line shows the number of hate crime incidents each year. This chart specifically shows hate crime incidents linked to ethnicity and national origin bias, from 1996 to 2014.

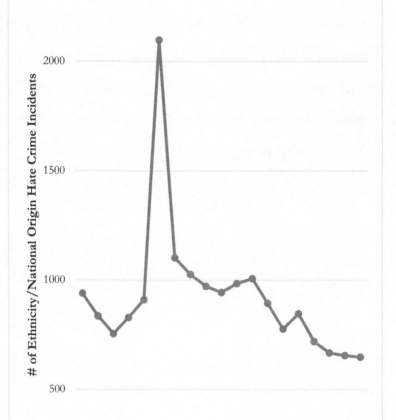

Disability Hate Crimes in the USA
(1997-2017)

The following chart is a representation of hate crimes in the USA from 1997 to 2017 based on data from the FBI. The line shows the number of hate crime incidents each year. This chart specifically shows hate crime incidents linked to physical and mental disability bias.

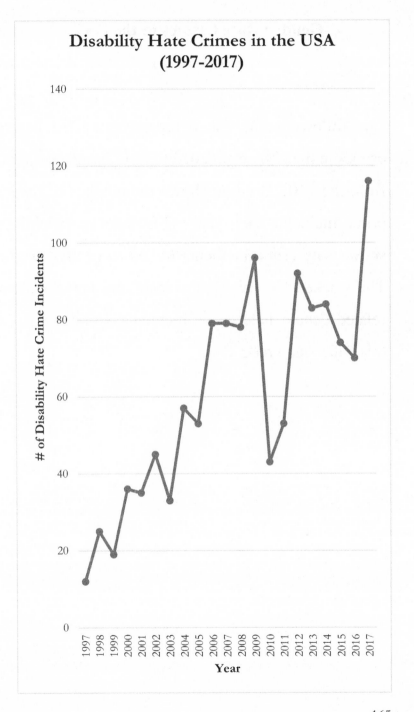

Gender Hate Crimes in the USA
(2013-2017)

The following chart is a representation of hate crimes in the USA from 2013 to 2017 based on data from the FBI. The line shows the number of hate crime incidents each year. This chart specifically shows hate crime incidents linked to gender bias. The stacked bars show anti-male and anti-female related gender hate crime incidents. Collection of this data began recently.

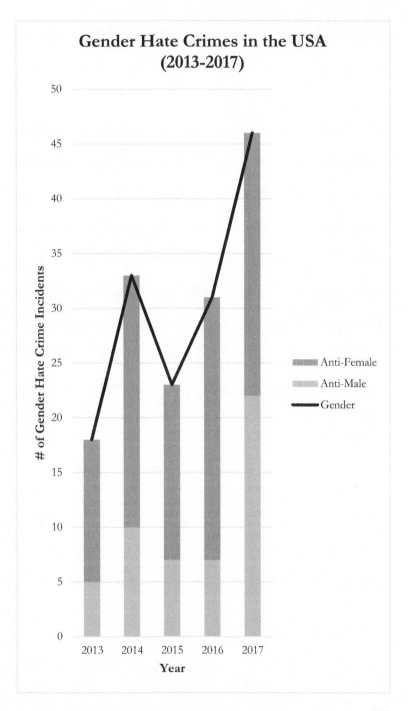

Gender Identity Hate Crimes in the USA (2013-2017)

The following chart is a representation of hate crimes in the USA from 2013 to 2017 based on data from the FBI. The line shows the number of hate crime incidents each year. This chart specifically shows the trend in the hate crime incidents related to gender identity bias. The two bars for each year plot data for anti-transgender and anti-gender non-conforming related hate crime incidents. Collection of this data began recently.

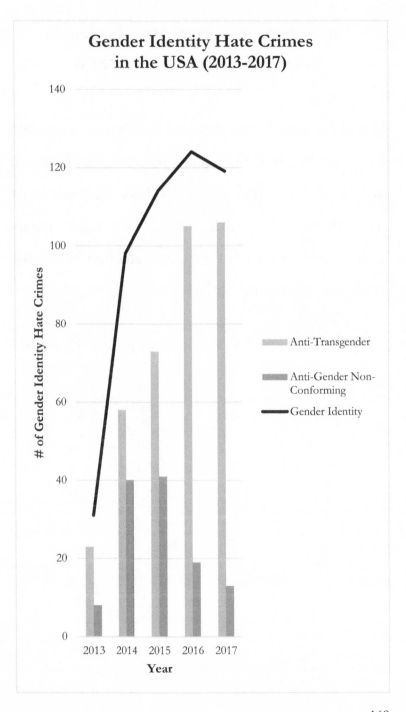

Hate Crimes and Motivating Factors in England and Wales (2011-2018)

Here I have included some of the charts using data from the Home Office for hate crimes in England and Wales. The line graph displays the number of hate crimes over time along with hate crimes categorized by motivating factor stacked below for each year from 2011 to 2018.

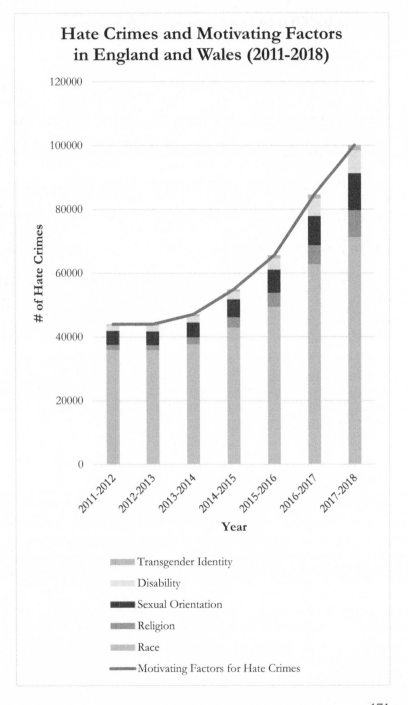

Hate Crimes and Motivating Factors in England and Wales (2011-2018)

Hate Crimes and Motivating Factors in England and Wales (2011-2018)

In this chart using data from the Home Office, the lines show the total number of hate crimes along with hate crimes sorted by motivating factor each year from 2011 to 2018. Most of the hate crimes were motivated by race.

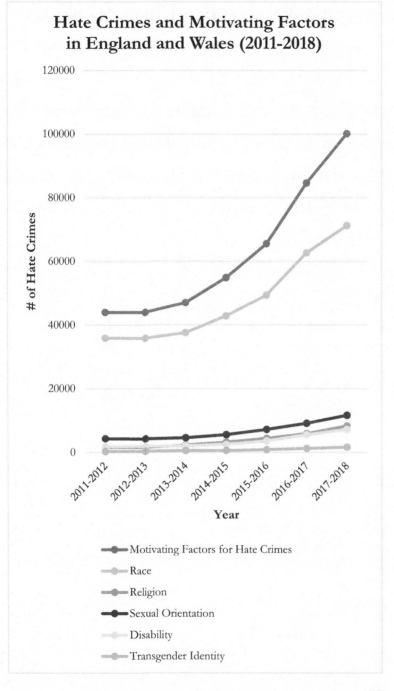

Hate Crimes and Motivating Factors in England and Wales (2011-2018)

Police-Reported Hate Crimes in Canada
(2014-2017)

In this chart using data from Statistics Canada, the line graph shows police-reported hate crimes in Canada over time along with hate crimes categorized by motivating factor stacked below for each year.

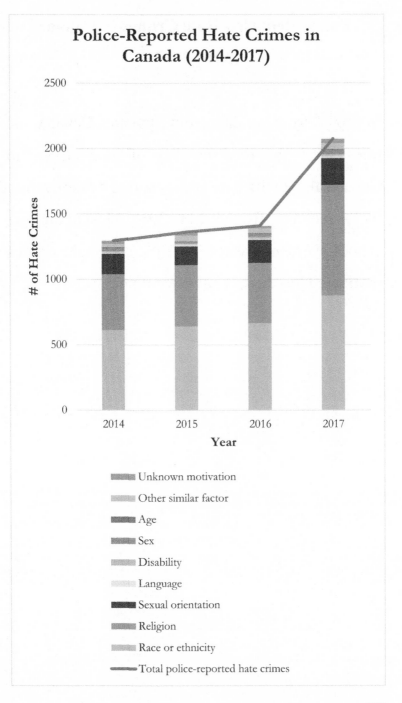

Police-Reported Hate Crimes in Canada
(2014-2017)

In this chart using data from Statistics Canada, the lines show the total number of hate crimes in Canada along with hate crimes sorted by motivating factor each year from 2014 to 2018. Most of the hate crimes were motivated by race, but hate crimes motivated by religion have been increasing.

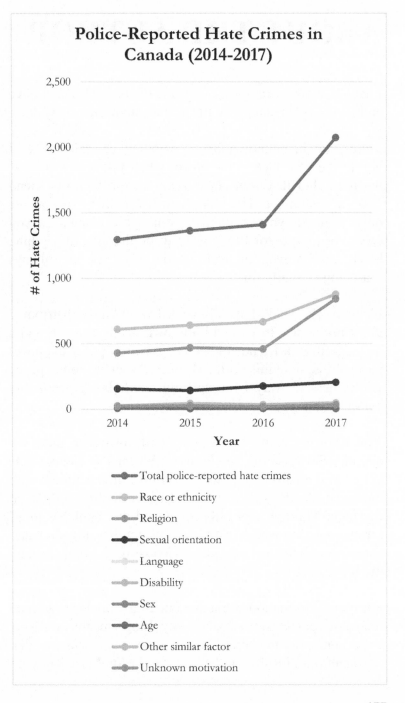

Police-Reported Hate Crimes in Canada (2014-2017)

ABOUT THE AUTHOR

I have lived the struggles, overcame the obstacles, as I have endured the pain and joy of life as they landed upon my door.

I like to be the unknown face to whom all can relate. I want you to see your face in the mirror when you search for me, not mine. For if it is my face in the mirror, then my friend you see a stranger. The unknown face is there so you see only yourself, your struggles, your achievements as you cross the journey of life. I want to be the face of a white, black, and brown, as well as the love we are always searching eternally for.

If this world would have allowed, I would have distributed all of my books, to you with my own hands as a gift and a message from a friend. I have taken pen to paper to spread peace throughout this Earth. My sacred soul has found peace within herself. May I through my words bring peace and solace within your soul.

You have my name and know I will always be there for anyone who seeks me. My home is Washington State, USA, yet I travel all around the world to find you, the human with humanity. Aside from my books, I love writing openly on my blog. Through this blog journey, I am available to all throughout this world. Come, let us journey together and spread positivity, as I take you on a positive journey through my blog.

For more information about any one of my books, or to read my blog posts, subscribe to my blog on my website, www.annmarieruby.com. Follow me on social media, @AnnahMariahRuby on Twitter, @TheAnnMarieRuby on

Facebook, @ann_marie_ruby on Instagram, and @TheAnnMarieRuby on Pinterest.

MY SPIRITUAL COLLECTION

I have published four books of original inspirational quotations:

Spiritual Travelers:
Life's Journey From The Past To The Present
For The Future

Spiritual Messages:
From A Bottle

Spiritual Journey:
Life's Eternal Blessings

Spiritual Inspirations:
Sacred Words Of Wisdom

For all of you whom have requested my complete inspirational quotations, I have my complete ark of inspiration, I but call:

Spiritual Ark:
The Enchanted Journey Of Timeless Quotations

180

Do you believe in dreams? For within each individual dream, there is a hidden message and a miracle interlinked. Learn the spiritual, scientific, religious, and philosophical aspects of dreams. Walk with me as you travel through forty nights, through the pages of my book:

Spiritual Lighthouse:
The Dream Diaries Of Ann Marie Ruby

When there was no hope, I found hope within these sacred words of prayers, I but call songs. Within this book, I have for you, 100 very sacred prayers:

Spiritual Songs:
Letters From My Chest

Prayers are but the sacred doors to an individual's enlightenment. This book has 123 prayers for all humans with humanity:

Spiritual Songs II:
Blessings From A Sacred Soul

MY LATEST BOOK

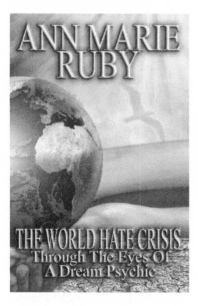

The World Hate Crisis: Through The Eyes Of A Dream Psychic

BIBLIOGRAPHY

"Alexander the Great." *AZQuotes.com*. Wind and Fly LTD, 2019. Web. 24 February 2019. <https://www.az quotes.com/quote/116036>

Eisenhower, Dwight D. "Second Inaugural Address of Dwight D. Eisenhower." *The Avalon Project*, Yale Law School Lillian Goldman Law Library. Web. 5 Feb. 2019. <http://avalon.law.yale.edu/20th_ century/eisen2.asp>

Gandhi, Mohandas K. *An Autobiography: The Story of My Experiments with Truth*. Translated by Mahadev H. Desai, Boston: Beacon Press, 1993.

"Hate Crime." United States Department of Justice, Federal Bureau of Investigation. Web. 05 Feb. 2019. <https://ucr.fbi.gov/hate-crime>

Hitler, Adolf. *Hitler's Table Talk, 1941-1944: His Private Conversations*. Edited by H. R. Trevor-Roper and Gerhard L. Weinberg. Translated by Norman Cameron and R. H. Stevens, New York: Enigma Books, 2007.

Home Office. "Hate Crime, England and Wales,
2017/18." GOV.UK. 16 Oct. 2018. Web. 05 Feb.
2019. <https://assets.publishing.service.gov.uk/
government/uploads/system/uploads/attachment_
data/file/748598/hate-crime-1718-hosb2018.pdf>

"Mahatma Gandhi." *AZQuotes.com*. Wind and Fly LTD,
2019. Web. 24 Feb. 2019. <https://www.az
quotes.com/quote/105849>

Mandela, Nelson. *Long Walk to Freedom: The
Autobiography of Nelson Mandela*. New York
City: Black Bay Books, 1995.

Mother Teresa. *Where There Is Love, There Is God: A
Path to Closer Union With God and Greater
Love for Others*. New York City: Doubleday
Religion, 2010.

Mother Teresa and Brian Kolodiejchuk. *Mother Teresa:
Come Be My Light: The Private Writings of the
Saint of Calcutta*. New York City: The Crown
Publishing Group, 2009.

"The Nobel Peace Prize Award Ceremony 2001."
NobelPrize.org, Nobel Media AB 2019. Web. 24

Feb 2019. <https://www.nobelprize.org/
prizes/peace/2001/award-video/>

"Plato." *A-Z Quotes*, Wind and Fly LTD, 2019. Web. 22
Feb. 2019. <https://www.azquotes.com/quote/
1248213>

Pope Francis. "MESSAGE OF POPE FRANCIS TO
MUSLIMS THROUGHOUT THE WORLD FOR
THE END OF RAMADAN ('ID AL-FITR)."
Vatican: the Holy See. Vatican Website. Liberia
Editrice Vaticana, 10 Jul. 2013. Web. 5 Feb.
2019. <http://w2.vatican.va/content/francesco/
en/messages/pont-messages/2013/documents/
papa-francesco_20130710_musulmani-
ramadan.html>

Reagan, Ronald. "Address at Commencement Exercises at
Eureka College." The Ronald Reagan Presidential
Foundation and Institute. Web. 5 Feb. 2019.
<https://www.reaganfoundation.org/media/
128700/eureka.pdf>

Rutte, Mark. "Churchill Lecture by Prime Minister Mark
Rutte." Government of the Netherlands. 13 Feb.
2019. Web. 24 Feb. 2019. <https://www.govern
ment.nl/documents/speeches/2019/02/13/churchill-

lecture-by-prime-minister-mark-rutte-europa-
institut-at-the-university-of-zurich>

Statistics Canada. "Table 35-10-0066-01 - Police-
reported hate crime, by type of motivation."
2019. Web. 05 Feb. 2019. <https://www150.
statcan.gc.ca/t1/tbl1/en/tv.action?pid=351000660
1>

Tagore, Rabindranath. *Personality*. London: Macmillan
and Co., Ltd., 1917.

Watson, J. B. *Behaviorism*. New York: People's Institute
Publishing Company, 1924.

"Winston Churchill." *AZQuotes.com*. Wind and Fly LTD,
2019. Web. 24 Feb. 2019. <https://www.az
quotes.com/quote/56424>

Made in the USA
Las Vegas, NV
29 December 2023

83642010R00125